Greeted

Blessed

Pierced

A FRESH LOOK AT MARY OF NAZARETH

Eva Burkholder

Favored, Blessed, Pierced is a wonderful reflection on the life of Mary of Nazareth. It presents her not as she is often known, as the blessed Mother of Jesus, but as an exemplary saint experiencing the grace of God with much to teach all of us. This step by step look at her life opens an array of opportunities to look at our own walk with God, a precious life example to guide us along the way. This book will enhance your devotional time with God as well as your devotion to Him.

—Darrell L. Bock
Executive director for cultural engagement,
Howard G. Henricks Center for Christian Leadership and Cultural Engagement and
senior research professor of New Testament studies,
Dallas Theological Seminary

Eva delves into Mary's life through Scripture. She traces what happens to Mary as she follows God's call on her life. Readers will be challenged by Mary's faith as she responds to the joys, confusions, and heartaches of life. Practical, insightful, and encouraging, this devotional will enrich your soul. I realized anew the power and simplicity of Mary's response to God, "I am the servant of the Lord. Let it be to me according to your word."

—Sue Eenigenburg
Director of women's ministry, Christar,
author of *Screams in the Desert* and *More Screams, Different Deserts*, and
co-author of *Expectations and Burnout* and
Sacred Siblings

It's good to take time to think deeply on things that we take for granted—to dwell afresh on Scripture we've known for years. In this devotional book, Eva has done us a great service in bringing to light things we've heard before but perhaps never considered. Refresh your perspective and your prayer life as you consider Eva's meditations on these well-loved verses.

—Gloria Furman
Author of *Missional Motherhood* and *Treasuring Christ When Your Hands Are Full*

Eva has done a terrific job of capturing Mary's story while simultaneously challenging ours. Her slow, deliberate pace enables us to intently look, listen, and reflect. In each lesson, readers engage with Scripture and a summary based on solid biblical research (I'm geeking on her word studies!), and they are challenged with thought-provoking questions. *Favored, Blessed, Pierced* is a study of a woman's life. Our life. Jesus has something to say to us here.

—Rev. Dr. Jackie Roese
Founder and president of The Marcella Project,
author of *She Can Teach, Lime Green, I'm Enough* and
co-author of *Relationshift*

When Eva Burkholder told me she wrote a Bible study on Mary, the mother of Jesus, I was intrigued. There are few studies written from an evangelical perspective featuring this woman, highly favored by God. I told her it simply had to be published! *Favored, Blessed, Pierced: A Fresh Look at Mary of Nazareth* isn't the stereotypical book on Mary. This one made me feel as if I was right there experiencing life with Mary. Not just the beginning and end of the story but the middle where life happened. I'm looking forward to reading through it again during the advent season.

—Kathy Carlton Willis
God's Grin Gal, coach, writer, and speaker,
author of *Grin with Grace*

Clearly there is MORE to know about the woman to whom God entrusted the raising of the Son of God, his Son … Mary, the mother of Jesus, the Son of Man! Eva Burkholder leads us into a significant opportunity for pondering the realities of this woman of God as she fulfilled her unique calling. And so, we gain courage and insight for following God fully into our own! There's MORE to enjoy about what it means to love and trust God as we see MORE about the life and faith of Mary of Nazareth.

—Wendy L. Wilson
Mission advisor for development of women,
Missio Nexus and
executive director of Women's Development Track

Dedication

To Lane and John-Mark

*who gave me the undeserved honor of being a mom
but also showed me that my identity was so much more.*

Table of Contents

Introduction

What did the women in Scripture do? How can their examples inform my life? Those questions motivated me to write a Bible study on women several years ago. I specifically chose those who are marginalized, ignored, whose images have been distorted, women who fought against injustice, and women seldom heard of.

Mary of Nazareth, the mother of Jesus, didn't seem to fit my criteria of misunderstood women, so I skipped her. I naively thought my yearly dose of Christmas pageants and Easter plays taught me all I needed to know about her. But then I received a request to speak at a Christmas event and decided to take a fresh look at Mary. As a result, I found so much in her life that I had previously missed. For fifty years, I had overlooked a significant woman in my Christian heritage.

I also shied away from Mary because of how she has been portrayed by some faith traditions. Yet I erred by giving her too little attention. We usually look at Mary during Jesus's birth and crucifixion but miss Mary in the middle. New Testament writers reference Mary more frequently than anyone else after Jesus, Paul, and Peter. Six books of the Bible describe her and devote more verses to her than any other woman.

Perhaps the best example of a radical disciple, we find Mary at every major event in Jesus's life. The writers of the Gospels preserved and recorded many details about Jesus only because Mary witnessed and testified of them.

Worldwide, much attention and many works of literature, art, and sculpture focus on Mary. Rev. Dr. David Handy, a PhD scholar on the Gospel of Luke, explains her prominence:

Traditionally, since ancient times, in liturgical churches (Lutheran and Anglican, as well as Catholic and Eastern Orthodox), the Blessed Virgin Mary is considered the greatest of all the saints, bar none. Greater than Francis of Assisi in the 13th century, or Saint Benedict (founder of the Benedictine order of monks) in the 6th century, or any other saint—male or female. Yet Mary never held any office of leadership in the church, never wrote a book or received any theological education, and never seemed to accomplish anything besides raising her family in a godly way.[1]

In this study, I do not address what others say about Mary. Instead, I look primarily at what Scripture says about her in the Gospels, imagine myself in her place, and discover how her example can enhance my journey with Jesus.

The reader could use this book as an advent devotional, a daily devotional, a character study with a group of spiritual friends, or simply as a quick read.

Through questions and a prayer after each entry, this study guides the reader to interact with the principles gleaned from Scripture. Extra verses are also provided for further study and meditation on the concepts presented. A suggested leader's guide follows the thirty-one entries.

This study has led me to appreciate and love the beautiful example of this favored, blessed, and pierced woman. I hope and pray that the Mary you see on the pages of Scripture and through my reflections will challenge and encourage you as she has done for me.

ONE

Ordinary

*In the sixth month of Elizabeth's pregnancy, God sent
the angel Gabriel to Nazareth, a town in Galilee, to a
virgin pledged to be married to a man named Joseph, a
descendant of David. The virgin's name was Mary.*

Luke 1:26–27

Two thousand years ago, a young girl had a divine encounter that changed the course of human history. God had not directly spoken to his people in over four hundred years. But at this specific moment in time, in the sixth month of her cousin's pregnancy, an angel appeared to Mary.

Mary called Nazareth home. This small town that bordered foreign territory produced no educated or important people. Mary and her fiancé, Joseph, had entered the legal and binding contract of engagement, as official as marriage, but without the full benefits of cohabitation. Unlike today, this serious commitment—usually made between the ages of twelve and sixteen—could only be dissolved through divorce. A contract had been signed and money had been exchanged. Celebrating the ceremony, building a home together, and starting a family would come a year later.[2]

While Mary could trace her lineage back to Israel's great King David, the royal blood running through her veins had long become insignificant, due to years of captivity and foreign domination of her people. Her soon-to-be husband, also of royal lineage through a different son of King David, was merely a carpenter. And Mary had not yet born sons. All this would make her a nobody in the eyes of people in her world: an ordinary, young, unmarried peasant girl.

I too am ordinary—a middle class, Caucasian, married, middle-aged mother. I have asked myself, "What qualifications do I have to write a book?"

Mary spurs me on because despite her lack of credentials, she fulfilled this prophecy from Isaiah 7:14: "Therefore the Lord himself will give you a sign: The virgin will conceive and give birth to a son, and will call him Immanuel." God knew her, saw her, and chose her for a unique commission.

REFLECTION AND DISCUSSION

How about you? What credentials can you claim?

Where do you come from?

What makes you unique?

Don't let your location, hometown, race, gender, financial status, family background, lack of education, marital status, or anything else cause you to feel disqualified to be called or used of God.

PRAYER

Lord, thank you that you used a lowly peasant girl. Thank you that my credentials do not disqualify me from encountering you and being commissioned by you. I trust that you will be faithful to fulfill your plans through me.

FURTHER STUDY

Psalm 8:3–8

Psalm 139:13–16

1 Corinthians 1:26–31

TWO

Greetings

*The angel went to her and said, "Greetings, you who are
highly favored! The Lord is with you." Mary was
greatly troubled at his words and wondered what kind
of greeting this might be.*

Luke 1:28–29

Troubled. Greatly troubled. Agitated and disturbed. Sounds
about right. Not often does a heavenly being speak to a
young peasant girl going about her daily business.

But surprisingly, Mary wondered—reasoned, deliberated,
considered—about his message, rather than about the
sudden appearance of an angelic being. She wondered at the
meaning of the greeting. What kind of greeting was this?

Putting myself in Mary's place, my thoughts would have
raced along these lines:

Why pick me, an ordinary girl?
Who am I to be favored? Surely you have the wrong person.
I've heard the stories and this kind of favor usually doesn't end well.
I'd rather remain anonymous.
What will I have to do?
What awaits me that I need God's presence?
I have a bad feeling about this.

Sometimes my response to God's call is like Elizabeth
Bennett's in Jane Austen's novel, *Pride and Prejudice*. She
replies to her sister Lydia's offer to find her a husband with,

"I thank you for my share of the favor, but I do not particularly like your way of getting husbands."[3] In these instances, I don't like the way God "favors" me, because I think his methods are flawed, as Lydia's were, instead of recognizing that his ways are always perfect.

Other times, I know that God's way is best, but like the proverbial call to missions, I assume he will send me to the farthest reaches of Africa instead of trusting he will lead me to a place suited for my talents and gifts.

Why do I always think the worst? That God's commission means something horrible, difficult, or the most dreadful thing I could imagine, when in fact his plans for me are based in his goodness?

"The Lord is good and has compassion on all he has made (Psalm 145:9). "The Lord is good, a refuge in times of trouble. He cares for those who trust in him (Nahum 1:7).

REFLECTION AND DISCUSSION

When God commissions you, what assumptions do you make?

What does this say about your view of God's goodness?

PRAYER

I thank you Lord for my share of your favor. You always have my good in mind, and you know what you're doing. Help me to trust you when you speak and not assume the worst right away, but rather remember your goodness.

FURTHER STUDY

Exodus 3:4–6, 11

Jeremiah 1:4–6

Acts 9:3–6

THREE

With You

But the angel said to her, "Do not be afraid, Mary."

Luke 1:30a

The angel's preface to his commissioning, "Do not be afraid," is the most commonly repeated command in the Bible—with good reason, for we are people of fear.

Last year, I finally admitted that I feel anxious when I travel. While I have the privilege of traversing the globe in my ministry to cross-cultural workers, I rarely travel alone. Still I worry. *Will we make the flight? Will we figure out the train? What if we don't have enough cash? Where do we get cash? Will we find our Airbnb? If we rent a car, will we know where to park? Where will we eat? What if we get lost?*

Fear causes us to make poor decisions, to react wrongly, to shy away from obedience; it keeps us from taking necessary risks. I've seen a quote attributed to Elisabeth Elliot that says, "Fear arises when we imagine that everything depends on us."

Mary's fear stemmed from the uncertainty of what the angel would ask her to do (although his terrifying presence probably added to it as well). But do not miss what the angel had already told her in verse 28, "The Lord is with you." These two phrases often accompany each other in Scripture.

To the Israelites: "Be strong and courageous. Do not be afraid or terrified because of them, for the Lord your God goes with you; he will never leave you nor forsake you" (Deuteronomy 31:6).

To Joshua: "Have I not commanded you? Be strong and courageous. Do not be afraid; do not be discouraged, for the Lord your God will be with you wherever you go" (Joshua 1:9).

To Isaiah: "So do not fear, for I am with you; do not be dismayed, for I am your God. I will strengthen you and help you; I will uphold you with my righteous right hand" (Isaiah 41:10).

And then to Mary, calling her by her name, God gave his personal promise that he would be with her no matter what she would face. Thus, she did not need to fear.

As I contemplated my anxiety about travel, I realized that I do eventually relax and enjoy the experience because my husband, Mark, accompanies me. As the adventurous one, he rents the cars, navigates the new directions and drives over one hundred miles an hour on the autobahn. And just as Mark's presence helps assuage my anxiety, God's presence overshadows my fear as well.

To me and to you, God says, "'Never will I leave you; never will I forsake you.' So, we say with confidence, 'The Lord is my helper; I will not be afraid. What can mere mortals do to me?'" (Hebrews 13:5b–6).

REFLECTION AND DISCUSSION

What are you afraid of?

What would you do if you had no fear?

In what ways have you sensed God's presence lately?

PRAYER

Father God, I list my fears: ________________________________.
I draw near to you. I press into your presence, becoming aware that you are with me. May your nearness overshadow my fear.

FURTHER STUDY

Psalm 118:5–7

Jeremiah 1:7–8

Philippians 4:5b–6a

FOUR

Favored

You have found favor with God. You will conceive and give birth to a son, and you are to call him Jesus. He will be great and will be called the Son of the Most High. The Lord God will give him the throne of his father David, and he will reign over Jacob's descendants forever; his kingdom will never end.

Luke 1:30b–33

Favor. Favor with God. In Greek, *charis*.[4] It means grace, the loving kindness of the merciful God.

The discovery of the meaning of this word startled me. I have always read this story thinking that God selected Mary because she possessed special qualities—humility, modesty, holiness, and faith. But after studying the word "favor," I now know I had it all wrong. God chose Mary solely by grace —the same grace that chooses you and me.

> Praise be to the God and Father of our Lord Jesus Christ, who has blessed us in the heavenly realms with every spiritual blessing in Christ. For he chose us in him before the creation of the world to be holy and blameless in his sight. In love he predestined us for adoption to sonship through Jesus Christ, in accordance with his pleasure and will—to the praise of his glorious grace, which he has freely given us in the One he loves. (Ephesians 1:3–6)

The NIV New Testament Commentary explains it like this: "Despite all her qualities, God's choice of Mary to bear his child springs from his grace, not from any inherent merit she possesses. She is the object of God's unmerited, graciously provided goodness. God acted on her behalf and not because of her."[5]

I used to believe that I just needed to follow Mary's example and God would choose me for some extraordinary purpose. Stuck in the Old Testament with obey-and-you-will-enter-the-promised-land as my *modus operandi*, I became the "good girl." I followed the rules so that all would go well with me and I might serve God in grand ways.

Now I see grace. I have favor with God because he adopted me as his child. My good or bad behavior doesn't determine God's favor. I received it through Christ's death.

Just as God gave Mary a special commission, God has selected us for some special purposes. The overarching ones call us all to action: rule and subdue (Genesis 1:28), make disciples (Matthew 28:19–20), love one another (John 13:34). But there are many smaller commissions throughout our lifetime, none of which we earn.

In Matthew 20, Jesus tells a parable about laborers who work for different lengths of time but receive the same pay. Author Pete Briscoe says this about our value of getting what we think we've earned:

> If you've been working for Christ, diligently doing his work for a long time, you will automatically identify with the guys who worked all day, complaining (probably to yourself) about why the last guys get the same as you. But that's not who you are in the passage. This passage is about the last person hired. In this story, you are the last person hired, the one who gets far, far more than he has

earned. And friends, this is the best news you could ever hear.[6]

God's grace invites Mary, and now us, to participate in this great task of building his kingdom—to be ready and willing to obey the commission when it comes.

REFLECTION AND DISCUSSION

On what basis do you expect that God will give you special assignments?

☐ *I have been faithful (sacrificial, patient etc.), therefore God should protect (reward, answer, etc.) me.*

☐ *I did God a favor, so I expect him to repay me with a favor.*

☐ *Since God has done me a favor, I must do one for him.*

☐ *I am not good enough for any favor from God.*

☐ *Other* ____

PRAYER

Gracious Savior, thank you for saving me by grace, accepting me, and choosing me to do good works for you. Thank you for the reminder that I don't deserve your assignments based on my behavior but, rather, based on your grace. I repent of my pride that causes me to think I deserve your favor.

Matthew 20:1–16

Ephesians 2:4–10

FIVE

Clarification

*Mary said to the angel, "How will this be, since I have
not had sexual relations with a man?"*

Luke 1:34 (NET)

How will this be? Mary needed more information. After all,
the angel was asking her to believe and participate in
something that transcended human experience, something no
one would believe or even imagine. Rather than doubting or
quarreling, she needed confirmation. She sought to
understand. So, she asked a clarifying question.

Clarifying questions seek additional information and keep the
speaker talking while helping the listener understand.

Clarifying questions look like this:

"I'm not quite sure I understand what you are saying."

"I don't feel clear about the main issue here."

"When you said that, what did you mean?"

In my job as a missionary member care provider, I work hard
at being a good listener. To that end, I try to ask more
clarifying questions and fewer curiosity questions.

Curiosity questions put the focus on me, not the speaker.
These queries ask for details I care about and send the
speaker off on tangents they might not want to talk about.

Instead, I desire to hear what the speaker wants to share and not just fish for what I'd like to know—thus clarifying questions are my goal.

Author Paul David Tripp addresses this in his book *Suffering: Gospel Hope When Life Doesn't Make Sense*. When you "come to God with sincere questions, asking is an act of faith. You're not rebelling against him; you're not running from him. You're not demanding answers but crying out of your confusion for the help that only he can give."[7]

This is the cry of many a believer caught in bewildering situations. At least ten times, the writers of the Psalms ask, "How long, O Lord?" Even Jesus asked of his Father God, "Why have you forsaken me?" (Matthew 27:46).

Like Mary, I also apply this principle in my listening to the Lord. I want to understand what he is saying to me, to make our conversations about him and not me, and to allow him to tell me what he desires to say, not just get him to say what pleases me. And when I am confused, I try to come with sincere questions in an act of faith.

REFLECTION AND DISCUSSION

When you listen to a friend, do you catch yourself seeking only the information you want to hear, or do you allow them to share as they desire? Explain.

What do your conversations with God look like? Are you a good listener? Do you demand answers or seek to understand?

PRAYER

Father God, teach me to listen to you, to make our conversations about you, to hear what you are trying to say to me. Teach me the art of asking sincere questions so I can be a better friend and listener to those around me.

FURTHER STUDY

Judges 6:12–18

Psalm 69:16–17

SIX

Impossible

*The angel replied, "The Holy Spirit will come upon
you, and the power of the Most High will
overshadow you. Therefore the child to be born will
be holy; he will be called the Son of God. And
look, your relative Elizabeth has also become
pregnant with a son in her old age—although she
was called barren, she is now in her sixth
month! For nothing will be impossible with God."*

Luke 1:35–37 (NET)

In answer to Mary's question, the angel essentially replied, "God's got this. This is a Holy Spirit thing." He reassured her that God could do the impossible. And then to prove it, he gave her a sign.

In three months, her cousin Elizabeth would become a mother. Elizabeth, the one who had never been able to get pregnant, had finally conceived. And in her old age, no less.

Surely Mary must have also remembered another ancestor, Sarah, who likewise bore a son when past childbearing age. Miraculous pregnancies dotted the history of Mary's people to reassure her that just as he had worked a miracle for Sarah and Elizabeth, so he would for Mary.

"Nothing will be impossible with God." Other translations say, "For no word from God will ever fail." This literally means that "not any word from God is without power."

Every word, every promise God speaks has power—enough power behind it to bring it to pass.

When Sarah heard God's promise of a son, she laughed. But God replied, "Is anything impossible for the Lord?" (Genesis 18:14 NET). And she gave birth to a son despite her unbelief.

Two women—one young, one old, one believed, one doubted—and yet God's words still came to pass. Sarah's unbelief did not nullify God's promise, nor did Mary's belief bring it about. If God promises, it will happen.

Both Sarah and Mary were great women, not because of belief or in spite of unbelief, but simply because God chose them. Sarah and Mary did not receive children because they asked for the impossible, but because God fulfilled his promises to them.

Whenever God asks me for the seemingly impossible, I need the reassurance God gave to Mary—the reminder of the other impossible things he has done. The births of my two sons count as a God thing. Preeclampsia, low birth weight, and a breech position necessitated cesarean sections with both. Their miraculous births encourage me. My faith also increases when I remember others who never carried a child in their womb but gave birth to dozens of spiritual children or birthed ministries against all odds.

And I am further heartened because even when my faith remains small, God remains faithful (1 Thessalonians 5:24).

REFLECTION AND DISCUSSION

What impossible thing has God spoken to you about?

What other impossible things has God done that can boost your faith?

What sign has God given you that his word will not fail?

PRAYER

Precious Lord, I adore you for being a God who does the impossible, whose words do not fail, who has power to fulfill his promises. I worship you for the miraculous things you have already done. Teach me more about you so I can believe and trust that when you make a promise, you will bring it to pass, no matter how impossible it seems to me.

FURTHER STUDY

Genesis 18:10–15

Numbers 23:19

Matthew 19:25–26

SEVEN

Let It Be

*And Mary said, "Behold, I am the servant of the
Lord; let it be to me according to your word." And
the angel departed from her.*

Luke 1:38 (ESV)

After receiving her commissioning and reassurance that God
would do the impossible, Mary responded with three
beautiful phrases.

First, "behold" (which we don't use these days) means "See!
Look! Here I am!" Picture students responding to a
classroom roll call: "Eva, Mark, Mary?"

"Yes. Here!" Ready and available.

Next, "I am the servant of the Lord" can be translated as
"Lord, I present myself to you." This continual prayer of
openness to God echoes the living sacrifice found in Romans
12:1: "Therefore, I urge you, brothers and sisters, in view of
God's mercy, to offer your bodies as a living sacrifice, holy
and pleasing to God—this is your true and proper worship."

And lastly, "Let it be to me" is Mary's voluntary wish that
God's commission be done to her. In essence, she replied, "I
wish for this. I sign up for it heart and soul."

By responding in this manner, Mary illustrates Ephesians
2:10: "For we are God's handiwork, created in Christ Jesus to

do good works, which God prepared in advance for us to do." God had favored (graced) her with a good work. She merely accepted.

I wonder at times how I can do the job God has given me—serving in a small mission agency with no formal counseling degree; trying to influence leaders (especially men) to consider protocols they might not naturally think about; bearing responsibility for whether or not a worker remains on the field; predicting preventable reasons for attrition; matching burned out and discouraged people with effective resources.

But then I look at Mary. She did not let any of the normal excuses hold her back. And she didn't yet have the resurrection of Jesus or the indwelling Holy Spirit to bolster her faith. She simply said, "Let it be."

I want that courage, that surrendered heart, that faith.

REFLECTION AND DISCUSSION

What task is God asking you to do?

Select your current response to this commission:

☐ *How will this be?*

☐ *I don't like my assignment. Got something else?*

☐ *My task is too small. I was made for bigger things.*

☐ *You have the wrong person. I can't do this.*

☐ *I don't know what to do. I'm just a follower.*

☐ *I don't deserve this.*

☐ *Let it be to me according to your word.*

PRAYER

Lord, I present myself to you. Here I am for whatever you would wish. (If you cannot say these words yet, ask God to help you say them. If you don't want to say them, ask God to help you want to say them. If you aren't even at that point yet, ask God to show you why it is good for you to say them.)

FURTHER STUDY

1 Samuel 3:10

Luke 1:48

Romans 6:18–19

EIGHT

Make It So

*And Mary said, "Behold, I am the servant of the
Lord; let it be to me according to your word." And
the angel departed from her.*

Luke 1:38 (ESV)

Mary's extraordinary response to her charge to birth the
Savior demands further examination. A little internet digging
led this amateur Greek sleuth to a rich gold mine of truth.

This simple phrase "let it be to me," is *genoito* in Greek (from
the root word *ginomai*). It means "to become, and signifies a
change of condition, state, or place."[8] A quick look at how
Greek verbs work is helpful in this case particularly. Greek
adds moods and voices as well as tenses to the verbs that we
do not have in English, and this gives us added clues to their
meanings.

In this case, the author of Luke has used the optative mood,
which indicates a wish or prayer of the speaker.[9] Secondly, he
used the middle voice to indicate that the subject of the verb
(Mary) is doing the action (changing her condition) for her
own benefit.[10] Putting these together, we get something like
this: "This is my voluntary wish that this be done to me—
that my condition change to be what you say."

In other words, Mary replied with a resounding yes to God.
We see her, in effect, saying, "I see what you are doing, Lord,
and I give myself heart and soul to your plan. I voluntarily
sign up."

The strength of Mary's response becomes more pronounced when we look at an expression used by the apostle Paul. In Romans 6:1–2, Paul examines the logic of sinning more to increase grace. In this passage, he uses *me genoito*—the opposite form of "let it be to me:"

> What shall we say then? Shall we go on sinning so that grace may increase? By no means [*me genoito*]! We are those who have died to sin; how can we live in it any longer?

Additional internet searching reveals the vehemence of Paul's expression. To demonstrate how much he refuses to accept this idea, he uses the strongest word possible—akin to a swear word. By no means! May it never be! Absolutely not! God forbid! No way! In outrageous indignation, Paul exclaims "[strong expression] NO!"[11]

With that insight, we can surmise that Mary's response was just as forceful. "Absolutely, unequivocally, [strong expression] YES! Bring it on!"

Mary's quick surrender of her will and future to God's plan brings me up short. Too many times, I respond to God's call with a timid, "Ok, if you want me to, I'll try," or "Well, if you insist, I don't think I can do it, but...."

Mary gave no list of buts, no conditions, no hesitation—just yes! And furthermore, that yes came before any explanation of the details, guarantee of the results, or assurance of the reactions of others.

When I read Mary's response, my mind immediately jumps to a well-known phrase spoken by Captain Picard from the *Star Trek: The Next Generation* TV show. Whenever he wished for something to happen, he simply said, "Make it so." With complete faith in her God, Mary replied, "Make it so." And following her example, so will I.

REFLECTION AND DISCUSSION

In what difficult area of your life have you been asking, "How will this be?"

How can you move toward a response of "let it be"?

PRAYER

Lord, as I look to the future, would you "make it so?" Please turn my "how can this be?" into "let it be." I surrender my will and believe that your plans are best. Sign me up for whatever you wish. Absolutely, unreservedly, utterly YES!

FURTHER STUDY

Isaiah 6:8

Luke 22:42

Romans 6:15

NINE

Safe Place

*At that time Mary got ready and hurried to a town in
the hill country of Judea, where she entered Zechariah's
home and greeted Elizabeth.*

Luke 1:39–40

*In the time of Herod king of Judea there was a priest
named Zechariah, who belonged to the priestly division
of Abijah; his wife Elizabeth was also a descendant of
Aaron. Both of them were righteous in the sight of
God, observing all the Lord's commands and decrees
blamelessly. But they were childless because Elizabeth
was not able to conceive, and they were both very old.*

Luke 1:5–7

Imagine with me what Mary might have done next:

Mary sat there trying to catch her breath. What had just happened? Had an angel really stood right in front of her a few moments ago? She involuntarily gazed at her stomach as her hand touched her garment. *I'm going to have a baby boy! Is he already in there? The angel said his name will be Jesus. This is the Messiah, the One who will save us all!*

Wait! Who will believe me? What should I do? Who should I tell? Oh no, what about Joseph? She panicked. *Will he understand?* The truth of these unusual events hit her full force. *I could lose Joseph. Surely, he won't divorce me or have me stoned? Oh, what will Mama and Papa say? How will I tell them?*

Then she remembered the voice of the angel. *Cousin Elizabeth is pregnant too. I must talk to her. She'll understand. I need Elizabeth. I will go to her. She'll know what to do.*

Mary made the necessary preparations as soon as she could and headed off to the home of Elizabeth and Zechariah. As she walked, her thoughts turned to Elizabeth. *Righteous Elizabeth has followed God's commands and decrees better than anyone I know. She has also endured so much because she has no children. Poor Elizabeth. She has heard every reason possible for her childlessness and has been given every remedy known to man. Imagine thinking that Elizabeth's infertility stemmed from sin! And what about that unprofitable idea that she try mandrake leaves like our ancestor Rachel did! But that will end soon. A miracle has happened. She's going to have a baby. Wait! Two miracles have happened. I'm going to have a baby too!*

Mary pushed herself to go as fast as she could to Elizabeth's home, her place of safety and comfort.

What a precious relationship Elizabeth and Mary must have had. I believe Mary's journey to Elizabeth at this unique time indicates the significant role her cousin had in Mary's life—not just a relative, but a friend, a mentor, a sister, a confidante, an encourager—all that Mary needed.

Mary needed someone with strong faith to believe her testimony. She needed someone who had personal experience with miracles and God's way of doing things. She needed someone to explain the changes about to take place in her body. Someone who would not shame her or disapprove. Someone who would not compare and be jealous but empower her. Author and teacher, Jackie Roese, explains just how perfectly Elizabeth met these qualifications:

> Elizabeth helped Mary see what Mary couldn't see in herself. She inspired Mary to embrace who she was and the rightness of what she was doing. Elizabeth dreamed of hope for Mary. Mary could have been overwhelmed, hopeless, and scared, but Elizabeth stood behind her and cheered, "Run, Mary, run!" Elizabeth closed ranks and declared, "I've got you. I'm for you. Mary, let's do this."[12]

As Mary needed a safe place, so do we. We all need people in our lives who accept and love us as we are, who allow us to be open and authentic without judgment. People who draw us closer to the person God wants us to be.

Pondering Mary's relationship with Elizabeth makes me wonder who I hurry to when I have a unique need and to whom I might become a place of safety.

REFLECTION AND DISCUSSION

Who do you have in your life:

Who lives rightly and follows God wholeheartedly?

Who has experienced the miracles of God and knows he can do the impossible?

Who will give you godly counsel and encourage you to hear and obey the voice of God?

Who will cheer you on and encourage you to fly free?

Who will not police you, shame you, or try to keep you in your lane?

And likewise, to whom can you provide a place of safety and comfort?

PRAYER

Lord God, thank you for giving Mary a place to run to in her time of need. Thank you for Elizabeth's godly example. Please provide this kind of friendship and mentoring for me and my siblings in Christ. Teach us how to be a place of strong safety and comfort for others.

FURTHER STUDY

Romans 1:11–12

1 Thessalonians 2:7–12

Titus 2:1–8

TEN

Theologian

Most Jewish girls did not have formal education nor access to theological books. Instead, they relied on the oral tradition of parents reciting the stories of their ancestors and memorizing words from the Old Testament, particularly the Psalms. From this conscious storehouse of knowledge, Mary composed one of the most beautiful songs in Scripture— The Magnificat. The theology in this song of glory—for that is the meaning of *magnificat*—reveals a deep, courageous faith.

Mary starts out by focusing on Yahweh, the covenant-keeping God, not on herself or the child in her womb. Most of her song simply describes the Mighty One, revealing an intimate knowledge of him.

Mary knows that God is mighty. He does great things. For her specifically, he performed a miraculous conception.

She knows that God is holy. He is the only pure, blameless God, without fault.

She understands that God is merciful. He shows his grace, not only to Mary by choosing her to be the earthly mother of his son, but also to anyone in any generation who acknowledges him.

Mary has learned that God is her provider. He fills her when she is hungry and needy.

She knows that God is good. He gives her good things—a son and the honor of raising him—but even better, he gives her a Savior.

Mary grasps that God is omnipotent. He performs powerful deeds, he scatters the proud, he removes rulers from leadership, and lifts up the humble, as he does for Mary.

She comprehends that God is just. He does not favor the wealthy and privileged. After all, he chose her.

Mary knows that God keeps his covenants. He remembers his promise to Abraham so long ago and continues to help Israel—now by sending the promised seed (offspring) to crush Satan's head (Genesis 3:15).

Mary's courage challenges me. Her reference to bringing down rulers was a prediction of the overthrow of current oppressive leaders by the promised Messiah. These were "fighting words"—words that could have caught the attention of Rome and landed her in deep trouble. She is brave, gutsy, tenacious, and a danger to the status quo.[13]

Mary's theology impresses me. Without twelve years of school, Bible college, or seminary, she expresses profound truths. I am especially drawn to her words: "he has filled the hungry with good things." A quick look at the original language tells me that the hungry could also be translated "the needy." That's me. And good things mean "pleasant, useful, upright, and pleasurable" things. I want those too.

In other words, Mary teaches me anew that my God is good, and he gives to me that which benefits me, even if it also brings pain. Mary's "good thing" brought about the cross. What was painful for her produced the best of all good things—the salvation of the world.

Because Mary views God correctly, she views herself correctly. Thus, she glorifies God and rejoices. She expresses humility and realizes the future impact of this miracle, that she will be called blessed up until the present day.

REFLECTION AND DISCUSSION

What characteristic of God encourages you today and why?

How has God shown his goodness to you?

PRAYER

Lord God, Mighty One, I so need the reminder of your goodness. I feel so needy. My neediness sometimes overwhelms those around me. But you have filled me with good things, and today I choose to focus on what I have in you and not on what I lack.

FURTHER STUDY

Psalm 146

ELEVEN

The Magnificat

Mary, in Luke 1:46–55, joins three other women in Scripture who spoke hymns to God: Miriam, Deborah, and Hannah (see Further Study below to read their songs). Today I add my voice to theirs. I join their chorus.

Mary: "My soul glorifies the Lord and my spirit rejoices in God my Savior."

Hannah: "My heart rejoices in the Lord."

Miriam: "Sing to the Lord, for he is highly exalted."

Deborah: "I, even I, will sing to the Lord; I will praise the Lord, the God of Israel, in song."

Today I feel like Mary and Hannah and Miriam and Deborah! I must lift my voice and my pen and praise the Lord. Today I rejoice in my God and my Savior! I feel a song rising in me!

Mary: "For he has been mindful of the humble state of his servant. From now on all generations will call me blessed."

Hannah: "In the Lord my horn is lifted high."

While I haven't been blessed in the same way as Mary, I still feel that God has taken notice of me—a lowly, ordinary woman seeking to serve him. His marvelous grace has been extended to even me.

Mary: "For the Mighty One has done great things for me."

Hannah: "There is no one holy like the Lord; there is no one besides you; there is no Rock like our God."

God has been listening to my prayers and I see the beginnings of real, concrete, tangible answers to the deep cry of my heart. His answer, his healing has been so gradual that at times it has seemed negligible. But lately, it has come with unreserved abundance! I have found no other source for answers, no one else who could do the work he has done.

Mary: "His mercy extends to those who fear him, from generation to generation."

Hannah: "He raises the poor from the dust and lifts the needy from the ash heap; he seats them with princes and has them inherit a throne of honor."

God's lovingkindness that I see given to Mary has been extended to me. He has withheld what I deserved and given me what is undeserved.

Mary: "He has performed mighty deeds with his arm."

Hannah: "I delight in your deliverance."

This kind of healing and change only comes from his hand. Only he can reframe an addicted life, renew a stuck mind, and reprogram a depraved heart.

Mary: "He has scattered those who are proud in their inmost thoughts. He has brought down rulers from their thrones but has lifted up the humble."

Hannah: "Do not keep talking so proudly or let your mouth speak such arrogance, for the Lord is a God who knows, and by him deeds are weighed. The bows of the warriors are broken, but those who stumbled are armed with strength."

At times my pride has led me to feel I deserved his attention and his immediate action to my desperate need. But God is teaching me to accept his ways in his time.

Mary: "He has filled the hungry with good things but has sent the rich away empty."

Hannah: "Those who were full hire themselves out for food, but those who were hungry are hungry no more."

He has been more than what my hungry heart has needed and even wanted. He has filled and satisfied my emptiness with himself.

Mary: "He has helped his servant Israel, remembering to be merciful to Abraham and his descendants forever, just as he promised our ancestors."

Hannah: "He will guard the feet of his faithful servants, but the wicked will be silenced in the place of darkness."

As God did not forget to show love, compassion, and mercy on the children of Israel, so he has not forgotten me. He has shown the same love to me. It hasn't been in the way I wanted or in the timeframe that suited me, but his love has always been there for me.

REFLECTION AND DISCUSSION

Pen your own magnificat—a song of glory—in the pattern of Mary.

PRAYER

Thank you, my Lord for the recent goodness and love I have experienced. I testify that this grace comes from your hand, and I want to give praise to the Mighty, Holy One!

FURTHER STUDY

Exodus 15:20–21

Judges 5:1–31

I Samuel 2:1–10

TWELVE

Blessed

*When Elizabeth heard Mary's greeting, the baby leaped
in her womb, and Elizabeth was filled with the Holy
Spirit. She exclaimed with a loud voice, "Blessed are
you among women, and blessed is the child in your
womb! And who am I that the mother of my Lord
should come and visit me? For the instant the sound of
your greeting reached my ears, the baby in my womb
leaped for joy."*

Luke 1:41–44 (NET)

*Blessed is she who has believed that the Lord would
fulfill his promises to her!"*

Luke 1:45

*From now on all generations will call me blessed, for the
Mighty One has done great things for me."*

Luke 1:48b–49a

Recently this memory popped up on my Facebook page: "He
gives me such joy, has so many talents, and loves Jesus. I am a
blessed mother."

And this from a coworker heading to the mission field for
the first time: "The entire journey went smoothly without
any delays, missing luggage, or other problems. What a
blessing!!"

And what about this from a commercial for high speed internet? "Slow Wi-Fi at home. Guess I'm studying at the gym tonight. #NOTblessed"

#blessed appears daily over social media. I too call myself blessed and sign my notes with "Blessings, Eva." And Mary is known in many circles as "The Blessed Virgin Mary."

Let me quote Inigo Montoya in the movie *The Princess Bride*, "You keep using that word. I do not think it means what you think it means."

We typically think God is blessing us when we can list the things that make our lives good. We also associate blessing with godliness or earning God's favor. We feel blessed when life treats us well, when we receive a prayed-for job or a new car sits in our driveway.

All of us know someone who experiences fewer blessings than we do. We've seen places where poverty, struggle, injustice, racism, and cruelty run rampant. So, what about when the refrigerator breaks down again? Or a friend gets cancer? Or our child walks away from God? Or we still haven't found a spouse? Does that mean we are not blessed?

When Elizabeth said, "Blessed are you among women, and blessed is the child in your womb," she used the word *eulogeo*. This Greek verb means "to invoke a benediction over" or "speak well of" Mary and the baby in her womb. It indicates what Elizabeth did. She recognized that God had graced Mary with a great honor—a favorable expression from God.

However, in Elizabeth's second sentence—"Blessed is she who has believed that the Lord would fulfill his promises to her!"—and in Mary's declaration of herself—"From now on, all generations will call me blessed"—they used a different word: *makarios*, an adjective. It means "happy or fortunate, truly well off" and describes those for whom everything is good. *Makarios* speaks of life in the kingdom of God and never refers to material or physical benefits.

Elizabeth emphasized the fact that Mary's belief put her in a state of being well off. And Mary declared herself to be fortunate because she recognized God's hand at work doing mighty things. She was blessed, not because she had the privilege of birthing and raising the Son of God, but because she believed God's word proclaimed through the angel—that God could do the impossible by giving her a son and that son would be the Savior.

We too are blessed when we believe that God will do what he says he will do.

We are blessed when we acknowledge the mighty things he does.

REFLECTION AND DISCUSSION

2 Peter 1:4 says, "he has given us his very great and precious promises." List some of them. (See Deuteronomy 7:9, Psalm 62:2, John 1:12 for examples.)

What words of God do you believe or not believe today?

PRAYER

Gracious Father, today I choose to believe the promises in your Word and acknowledge the impossible, mighty things you do on my behalf. In that I am fortunate and well off.

FURTHER STUDY

Joshua 21:45

John 20:29

Romans 4:20–24

THIRTEEN

In the Kingdom

Blessed are the poor in spirit, for theirs is the kingdom of heaven.

Matthew 5:3

The Jews of Jesus's day had strict criteria for those they considered blessed by God. They had to be 100% Jewish, male, religious law keepers, wealthy, and have no physical ailments. By these standards, Mary would not have qualified as "The Blessed Mother," the one to give birth to the Messiah. Even though Jewish and religious (and presumably healthy), Mary's poverty and gender disqualified her.

But Jesus turned that thinking upside down. In the Sermon on the Mount (Matthew 5:3–10), Jesus "looked out at the crowd of desperate, sad, broken, and persecuted people, and called them makarios."[14] He invited women, the handicapped, the penniless, the half-Jew, the marginalized, and the immigrant into his kingdom.

James Bryan Smith, in his book *The Good and Beautiful Life: Putting on the Character of Christ*, describes true blessedness this way:

> The life circumstances that Jesus called blessed are commonly thought to be anything but that. And the Beatitudes are radical because they teach that these people have the same access to the kingdom as the rich and happy.[15]

Just like all who heard his message, Jesus invited Mary into his kingdom. And we know that Mary accepted the invitation of her son—the Son of God—because she attended the prayer meeting that birthed the church:

> When they arrived, they went upstairs to the room where they were staying. Those present were Peter, John, James and Andrew; Philip and Thomas, Bartholomew and Matthew; James son of Alphaeus and Simon the Zealot, and Judas son of James. They all joined together constantly in prayer, along with the women and Mary the mother of Jesus, and with his brothers. (Acts 1:13–14)

I succumb to the same faulty thinking as the Jewish leaders in Mary's day. I let their criteria feed my sense of superiority or at times my inferiority. I forget what Mary shows us: true blessing doesn't come from pedigree, or education, or gender, or wealth, or social status.

Instead, we are blessed because the kingdom—and Jesus himself—is available to us. We are blessed when we accept his invitation to become its citizens.

REFLECTION AND DISCUSSION

What criterion do you typically rely on in order to feel blessed?

What is your response to knowing you have been invited into God's kingdom?

PRAYER

King of heaven, thank you for inviting everyone into your kingdom. Thank you that I do not have to be wealthy and put together before I can join. Thank you that you include the poor, the sick, the marginalized, and the hurting. Thank you that you took Mary. Thank you that you took me.

FURTHER STUDY

Matthew 5:3–11

Note other reasons we are *makarios*:

- Luke 6:22

- Acts 20:35

- Romans 4:7–8

- 1 Corinthians 7:40

- 1 Peter 3:14

- Revelation 19:9

FOURTEEN

Hear and Obey

As Jesus was saying these things, a woman in the crowd
called out, "Blessed is the mother who gave you birth
and nursed you." He replied, "Blessed rather are those
who hear the word of God and obey it."

Luke 11:27–28

Once while Jesus was casting out a demon, the religious leaders accused him of getting his power from Satan. He sharply rebuked them with impressive words about Beelzebul and evil spirits taking up residence in a clean house (Luke 11:14-26).

Among the listeners stood an unnamed woman. Jesus's ability to answer and refute the religious leaders moved her to the point of calling out to him, "What a fortunate—*makarios*—mother you have."

I wonder if Mary also listened in the crowd that day? Did she hear this woman praise her, and did she feel vindicated? At last someone had acknowledged her. Finally, someone had said what any mother would want to hear, had given her recognition that she had raised a good son. This affirmation would have been especially meaningful because in those days, a woman's value proceeded from birthing and raising honorable sons.

I understand if Mary felt that way, because God revealed my heart recently regarding my own son. After a particularly difficult season, he experienced a transformation. As he recounted his journey with Jesus, I thought, *I prayed for that. God has answered my prayer!* But then he continued to tell me about a friend (who, incidentally, he later married) who prayed more specifically than I did, and her more detailed prayer had been answered.

And then I felt a twinge—an oh-so-subtle twinge. Was it disappointment? Jealousy? Whatever it was, it was ugly, because it meant I couldn't take credit for praying, and I realized I wanted to.

Something vaguely deceptive happens when we pray for a child, and then when God answers that prayer, we take credit for it ourselves. It happens when we raise our kids right, pray for them, see them make good decisions, watch them follow Jesus—and then think we are behind it. It's when we think our kids are following Jesus because of us.

If Mary was like me, she probably expected Jesus to heartily agree with the woman who called her blessed. But instead Jesus replied that she, "The Blessed Virgin Mary," was not the blessed one! Rather, the one who heard the word of God and obeyed was blessed. Jesus focused not on Mary but on hearing and obeying God's word.

The apostle James emphasizes this same concept: "But whoever looks intently into the perfect law that gives freedom, and continues in it—not forgetting what they have heard, but doing it—they will be blessed in what they do" (James 1:25).

Mary was blessed, not because she was Jesus's mother, but because she heard his word and obeyed. And she indicated this when she responded to the angel's commission, "I am the servant of the Lord; let it be to me according to your word" (Luke 1:38 ESV), and she became a disciple of the kingdom of God.

Likewise, my true blessings don't derive from any part I play in my son's choices or accomplishments, but in my obedience to God instead.

We are blessed when we respond in obedience to God's Word.

REFLECTION AND DISCUSSION

What reputation or accomplishments lead you to feeling falsely or wrongly blessed?

What words of the Lord are you obeying or do you need to obey?

PRAYER

King of heaven, teach me to obey you. Teach me to care more about your commands than about my reputation, or value, or my children's accomplishments. Help me find blessing in obedience, rather than in having perfect children.

John 13:17

Revelation 1:3

Revelation 22:7

FIFTEEN

True Identity

*As Jesus was saying these things, a woman in the crowd
called out, "Blessed is the mother who gave you birth
and nursed you." He replied, "Blessed rather are those
who hear the word of God and obey it."*

Luke 11:27–28

As a young girl, I thoroughly expected to become a mother
when I grew up. Getting an education or a degree was a
sideline, just in case marriage and motherhood didn't work
out. The role of parenthood receives much attention in my
Christian circles, so much so that my single siblings-in-Christ
wonder if God has overlooked them or if they committed
some gross error to prevent this expected "blessing."

When the unnamed woman in the audience affirmed Mary,
this would have been the perfect opportunity for Jesus to
praise the role of motherhood. After all, Mary nursed Jesus,
weaned and potty trained him, fed, and clothed him. And
greater still, she taught him how to act rightly and to know
and love God. She taught him his first theology. Rev. Dr.
David Handy explained it this way:

> Jesus too, although he was also divine, had to learn
> how to talk and read and write and do math or
> carpentry properly (none of which is innate or
> instinctive, but requires training). In all that sort of
> training, Mary would've played the most important
> role. [She had] more influence, humanly speaking,

over the kind of person [Jesus] became than any other person ever would or could have.

I don't think Jesus meant to diminish the role of motherhood. Rather, he wanted to emphasize that being his mother was not Mary's primary role or her main identity. Her identity was the same as it is for all women today—married or single, childless or bearing children, old or young, widowed or divorced, Indonesian or Scandinavian.

Women bear the image of God, representing his heart to the world (Genesis 1:27). Women are *ezer warriors*[16]—strong helpers or allies in battle—partnering with the men in their lives (Genesis 2:18). And together they rule and subdue the earth by building the kingdom as disciples of Jesus (Genesis 1:28). Carolyn Custis James, who coined the phrase *ezer warrior*, explains it best:

> A woman's life is truly blessed not when she becomes a mother, but when she hears and obeys his Word. The crowning glory for a woman (as for a man) is to be a disciple of Jesus Christ. This is a woman's true identity, and the only path to blessedness.[17]

One year, I had the privilege of watching my oldest son perform with his college choir at their Christmas concert. I so enjoyed his enthusiasm, the way he sang so heartily and paid full attention to the director. But then, to my surprise, he suddenly burst into a solo, confident and clear.

I beamed. I wanted the world to know he was my son. I posted bragging rights on social media. Later, at his senior recital, his professors testified to his character and maturity. However, Mary's example teaches me that, while I am proud of my son, I cannot rest on the laurels of his achievements or find my value in him. As Jesus defined Mary's identity, Jesus defines mine.

We are blessed when we recognize our identity is not in whose mother we are (or in being a mother at all) but in being a disciple of Jesus.

REFLECTION AND DISCUSSION

What defines your identity?

According to Jesus's definition, how are you blessed?

How do Jesus's words to his mother challenge your own sense of what gives you meaning and identity?

PRAYER

Lord God, while I am grateful to be a mother, thank you for showing me this is not my primary identity. Like all women (and men) everywhere, I am first of all your image bearer, and as that, I get to fight for your kingdom and serve you alongside my brothers.

Luke 10:17–20

Galatians 3:28

1 John 3:1

SIXTEEN

Be Grateful

Give thanks in all circumstances; for this is God's
will for you in Christ Jesus.

1 Thessalonians 5:18

Being blessed is not just giving God credit for our prosperity. It is not God rewarding us when we have faith or obey or act right. Blessedness is our state of being when we obey, believe, or display the characteristics of kingdom life—we are well off, we are *makarios*.

So, what do we do with *#blessed* when we see it on social media? What about all the good things in our lives? If we can't call them blessings, how do we acknowledge them?

Practice gratitude—an important discipline. Secular research proves what God has said to be true; gratitude can improve our mood and our wellbeing.

Jesus didn't acknowledge Mary when the random woman in the crowd wanted to praise her for raising such a great son. While Scripture doesn't record Mary's response at this moment, I wonder if she remembered what she had said in her song—that all generations would call her blessed? Here she was already experiencing the fulfillment of those words, and she gave praise to God for bestowing grace on her.

God's grace gave me my sons, and God's grace enables them to have talents and give me joy. God creates, calls, and saves my children. Everything stems from grace. Grace that I even found Jesus. Grace that he gave me a son. Grace that my son now chooses to follow Jesus.

God's grace lifts the burden during the times that I do all I can and my children still choose not to follow Jesus. Or when life doesn't turn out the way I expected. Or when I don't feel blessed. I pray, I love, and I let God's grace take over. I am challenged to simply be grateful and give God all the credit.

Now, instead of telling others "you are a blessing to me," I try to be more specific and choose my words with sensitivity. In doing so, I don't imply that God loves me more or less than someone else because I have been given different material possessions or relationships. I tell them, rather, how they have encouraged, challenged, helped, or inspired me. I tell them I am grateful for them.

Thank God for your husband and children, your childlessness, your singleness, your joys, and also your sorrows. Recognize the true source of all good things. Acknowledge where they come from, steward them well, and be content with what you have. Be grateful that even when bad things happen, you are still blessed by God's definition.

REFLECTION AND DISCUSSION

Start to list the things you are grateful for. When you default to saying "#blessed," reframe that statement to express gratitude and remind yourself what true makarios *is.*

PRAYER

Thank you, Lord God, for the good life you give to me out of your generous grace. I have many comforts that I do not earn, nor do I deserve. You are so gracious.

FURTHER STUDY

Psalm 100:4–5

1 Corinthians 1:4

Colossians 2:6–7

Colossians 3:15–17

SEVENTEEN

Pierced

Then Simeon blessed them and said to Mary, his mother: "This child is destined to cause the falling and rising of many in Israel, and to be a sign that will be spoken against, so that the thoughts of many hearts will be revealed. And a sword will pierce your own soul too."

Luke 2:34–35

I have already mentioned my propensity toward obedience and compliance. From a young age, I wanted to please my parents and teachers. I followed the rules, excelled in school, and received leadership roles. I also tried my best to obey God. For me, this meant pursuing Christian education, marrying a seminary graduate, going to the mission field, and serving together in ministry. I believed that if I was good, I would experience less trouble and God would reward me. I did not realize until much later that my good life was motivated not by the desire to love God, but by the desperation to avoid pain.

My life worked pretty well until I began to experience suffering. As a new bride, severe disappointment took root in my heart and developed into deep hurt—so deep I couldn't even speak it to myself, let alone out loud. As my disappointment and hurt grew, it blossomed into indignation. I felt as though I suffered unjustly. I had obeyed God, been a good Christian, walked the narrow path, and certainly did not deserve this.

Mary and Joseph took their forty-day-old Jesus to the temple to dedicate him and offer sacrifices to the Lord according to their custom and law. While there, a righteous man named Simeon recognized Jesus as the promised Messiah he had been waiting for all his life. Simeon's words of praise ended with an ominous prophecy for Mary, "A sword will pierce your own soul too." What a jolt of fear those words must have put in Mary's heart.

Typically, we think of Simeon referring to the way Mary's son would die. But as I have looked at Mary's life, I find pain all along her journey. Though favored and blessed, Mary was also pierced.

When Mary declared herself to be a slave of the Lord in Luke 1:28, she agreed to accept whatever God brought her way—good and bad, laughter and tears, joy and pain, life and death. There would be surface hurt and soul-searing pain. Some piercings would last a moment and others a lifetime.

I had to learn that obedience is not an elixir against pain. Everyone suffers in various ways because sin has affected our world (Romans 5:12). Matthew 5:45 says that the sun shines and the rain falls on both the righteous and the unrighteous. Are we alive? Do we breathe? Our soul will be pierced at some time in some way.

We know that Jesus entered our broken world so he might save it. But doing that meant a bloody battle against a powerful enemy. God, in accordance with his gracious character, gave Mary a heads-up, a kind of warning. This way, when the battle heated up with unexpected twists and turns, Mary would know God was still in control.

We too have been given a heads-up. 1 Peter 4:12–13 says, "Dear friends, do not be surprised at the fiery ordeal that has come on you to test you, as though something strange were happening to you. But rejoice inasmuch as you participate in the sufferings of Christ, so that you may be overjoyed when his glory is revealed."

May we, like Mary, declare ourselves to be God's servant even if it means a sword will pierce our soul too.

REFLECTION AND DISCUSSION

What might be stopping you from becoming a devoted servant of the Lord? Stop and talk to God honestly about your hesitation.

What has been your reaction to the trials you have experienced?

PRAYER

Lord, as Mary did, I declare that I am your servant. You have set me free from sin and death and made me a slave to righteousness and life. Empower me to serve you and trust that you know what you are doing even when my soul is pierced.

FURTHER STUDY

Romans 6:17–18

Romans 8:17

Philippians 2:5–8

EIGHTEEN

Upended

This is how the birth of Jesus the Messiah came about:
His mother Mary was pledged to be married to Joseph,
but before they came together, she was found to be
pregnant through the Holy Spirit.

Matthew 1:18

The saying goes: "The best laid plans of mice and men often go awry" (from *To a Mouse*, a poem by Robert Burns). Or to quote the true source: "Many are the plans in a person's heart, but it is the Lord's purpose that prevails" (Proverbs 19:21).

From the onset, Mary's favor and blessing mingled with her pierced soul. All set to marry Joseph and raise a normal Jewish family in Nazareth, her short encounter with the angel upended her plans. With her unexpected pregnancy, the normal order of life she had imagined changed in an instant. And any change of plans takes readjusting, rethinking, and dying to dreams.

While spiritually mature for her age and with a deep faith, Mary was still human. She probably expected to follow in her mother's footsteps. Or perhaps she dreamed of how she would keep her kitchen, raise her children, and organize her days. Maybe she hoped for a daughter to help her in the home.

Yet Mary responded to this sudden interruption to her expected life with surrender: "Let it be to me according to your word" (ESV), and praise: "The Mighty One has done great things for me—holy is his name."

I remember sitting in a team meeting with tears flowing down my cheeks. I could not shake the strong sense I had that life would never be the same, that I would never again be with this group of people in this room. God was nudging my husband and me to leave our ministry of twelve years. It didn't happen in an instant, but life did change. I had prepared to serve in Indonesia until I retired. I didn't make it past the age of forty. Upended. Pierced.

Our plans can go awry with no warning. A cancer diagnosis, children struggling, a spouse not finding the right fit, a parent's failing health, the loss of a partner, a permission denied, or a job lost.

Even when we know that God is redirecting us, it still pierces. Feeling this pain doesn't mean we don't trust God. It means we have to surrender and praise with the psalmist: "He alone is my protector and deliverer. He is my refuge; I will not be upended" (Psalm 62:2 NET).

REFLECTION AND DISCUSSION

What sudden loss of dreams or change of plans have you experienced?

How can you respond with surrender and praise?

PRAYER

Lord Jesus, thank you that while we make plans, your purposes prevail. When my plans are upended, I take refuge in you. In you my soul will not be shaken.

FURTHER STUDY

Psalm 62

NINETEEN

Misunderstood

*Because Joseph her husband was faithful to the law,
and yet did not want to expose her to public
disgrace, he had in mind to divorce her quietly.*

Matthew 1:19

Enter the fiancé. Joseph had to be told the fantastical story that Mary carried the Messiah in her womb and had conceived him by the Holy Spirit. While we don't know how she broke the news to him, we do know he struggled. He wanted a divorce but without humiliating Mary. Note the two phrases: "faithful to the law" and "public disgrace."

The law that Joseph referred to stated: "If a man happens to meet in a town a virgin pledged to be married and he sleeps with her, you shall take both of them to the gate of the town and stone them to death" (Deuteronomy 22:23–24a).

Because we know the rest of the story, we tend to skip over how Mary must have felt as she waited for Joseph to respond. Even if only for one day, she bore the pain of her fiancé not believing her and wanting to divorce her. Misunderstood. Pierced.

We all want those whom we love the most to believe us. When I explained our decision to return to the States from the mission field, I wanted others to know we had based our decision on clear Scripture and sound counsel and not on personal whim or comfort. But family and friends still suspected our motives: "Are you sure it's God you're hearing? Have you completed your task? Why would God call you away from the place of such great need?"

Mary's story didn't end there:

> *But after he had considered this, an angel of the*
> *Lord appeared to him in a dream and said, "Joseph*
> *son of David, do not be afraid to take Mary home*
> *as your wife, because what is conceived in her is from*
> *the Holy Spirit."… When Joseph woke up, he did*
> *what the angel of the Lord had commanded him*
> *and took Mary home as his wife.*
>
> *Matthew 1:20, 24*

Joseph married Mary immediately. The fear of rejection gone. A husband and father provided. Protection for her and her unborn son. Total understanding.

All my life, I have heard and believed that Mary was also misunderstood by her community as an unwed, pregnant woman. Dr. Timothy Ralston of Dallas Theological Seminary sheds new light on this and explains the significance of Joseph's willingness to take Mary and the baby as his own: "There is no clear indication anywhere within the New Testament that Mary was considered to have behaved immorally or that Jesus was illegitimate … Rabbinic teaching after the New Testament also allowed for pre-wedding sexual intercourse between bride and groom (if it occurred within her father's house) … Many years later, people called Jesus 'Joseph's son' (Luke 4:22). And as Joseph had hoped, Mary suffered no 'shame'—no ostracism from family, community, or religious leaders for her pregnancy." Ralston says some commentators speculate that the Jewish leaders made a veiled reference to Jesus's illegitimacy when they responded, "We were not born of fornication" (John 8:41 NKJV), but that this is unlikely based on context.[18]

In my case, time has shown how God took all the questions and the twists and turns of our return to the States and used them to make me an effective caregiver for other global workers. If God has directed you, entrust yourself to him. If you are misunderstood, remember, "So then, those who suffer according to God's will should commit themselves to their faithful Creator and continue to do good" (1 Peter 4:19).

REFLECTION AND DISCUSSION

In what ways have you been misunderstood when you followed God's leading?

What was your response, and how can you trust God to do the explaining?

PRAYER

Lord God, I entrust myself to you, the One who judges justly. When misunderstood, help me to stay steadfast to you and continue to do good.

FURTHER STUDY

2 Corinthians 1:12–14

1 Peter 2:19–23

TWENTY

At Risk

So Joseph also went up from the town of Nazareth in Galilee to Judea, to Bethlehem the town of David, because he belonged to the house and line of David. He went there to register with Mary, who was pledged to be married to him and was expecting a child. While they were there, the time came for the baby to be born, and she gave birth to her firstborn, a son. She wrapped him in cloths and placed him in a manger, because there was no guest room available for them.

Luke 2:4–7

"I can feel that," I told my obstetrician as he pricked the left side of my abdomen on December 11, 1992. Lying on an operating table in an outdated birthing clinic in Bandung, Indonesia, I waited for the epidural to take effect for a cesarean section. As with my first pregnancy, I again had preeclampsia, but this baby was also breech.

Finally, the doctor resorted to an additional local anesthetic and began the procedure. "What was that?" I gasped in my grogginess some time later.

"Your anesthetic is wearing off. Breathe with me," my teammate, a nurse, stated calmly.

Mercifully, a third dose of anesthesia took effect quickly, and I delivered a healthy son.

A year later, I miscarried a baby at twelve weeks—on my thirty-first birthday. During the night, I wept as I said goodbye to my third child. I didn't know it then, but I would never conceive again.

According to the World Health Organization, about 830 women die from preventable complications related to pregnancy or childbirth each day.[19] Childbirth always involves pain, whether from labor contractions or the scalpel. It has been and continues to be very dangerous. Giving birth was no exception for Mary.

Mary and Joseph traveled to his ancestral home, a journey of about eighty to ninety miles. And while pregnant, she most likely walked the three to four days it took to get there since a donkey is not mentioned in the narrative.

Upon arrival, they would have gone directly to the home of relatives only to find it already overflowing with others in town for the census. No eastern culture would turn family away, so Mary and Joseph were probably relegated to the ground level or an adjacent room that housed the livestock.[20]

Mary was young and this was her first delivery. She labored in pain. She would have known that many women died giving birth and her birthing situation was less than ideal. An animal shelter. She had no sterile birthing room. No registered nurse. No obstetrician. No anesthesia. No Lamaze class. At risk. Pierced.

Mary did the only thing she could do under those circumstances. She "believed that the Lord would fulfill his promises to her" (Luke 1:45). God had said she would have a child, and so she pushed through the piercing pain of labor. Joy intermingled with pain. Tears with laughter. And the Son of God was brought into the world.

For Mary, the pain of childbirth led to the joy of welcoming a son. But for some women, the pain ends in a pierced heart, empty arms, and dashed hopes. And many women around the globe understand the fear of giving birth in less than ideal circumstances. Still others never have the chance to give birth at all.

Whatever the outcome or the makeup of our family, Mary's example of belief reminds us that God is still faithful. "Know therefore that the Lord your God is God; he is the faithful God, keeping his covenant of love to a thousand generations of those who love him and keep his commandments" (Deuteronomy 7:9).

REFLECTION AND DISCUSSION

What risks are you taking to answer God's call?

Who or what have you birthed that has brought both joy and pain?

What promises of God can you trust today?

PRAYER

Faithful, covenant-keeping God, show your steadfast love to women everywhere whose childbirth experiences have not ended in joy. Today we remember your promises, and we believe that you love us.

FURTHER STUDY

Psalm 145:13

Galatians 4:19–20

Philippians 2:30

TWENTY-ONE

Compelled

*So [the shepherds] hurried off and found Mary and
Joseph, and the baby, who was lying in the manger.
When they had seen him, they spread the word
concerning what had been told them about this child,
and all who heard it were amazed at what the
shepherds said to them. But Mary treasured up all
these things and pondered them in her heart. The
shepherds returned, glorifying and praising God for
all the things they had heard and seen, which were
just as they had been told.*

Luke 2:16-20

Imagine with me the shepherds' conversation after receiving
the message from the angels (Luke 2:8-15).

> "Quick guys, this way. Run, keep up. Over here.
> We've found him—the Messiah. Just like the angel
> said—wrapped in cloths and lying in a manger."

> "Wow, this little one is the Savior of the world. And
> we get to see him!"

After seeing the child:

> "We cannot keep this to ourselves. Let's tell others
> so they will know the one we have been praying for
> has finally arrived. Everyone needs to know that the
> Savior has come."

Imagine Mary's response.

> "What just happened? Was I dreaming? His perfect little face looks so normal. He must really be the Savior as the angel told Joseph and me. These shepherds have confirmed it. A whole lot of angels spoke praises to God. They said peace will come to those on whom God's favor rests. I think that includes me and Joseph and my child. How amazing. How unexplainable. Surely God orchestrated this moment; I want to always remember it."

I wonder if Mary saved a piece of the cloth and dried some straw as a memorial? Now the shepherds respond again:

> "Hey, friends, listen to our news. We have just seen the Savior. Praise God. He has kept the promise he made many years ago. A bunch of angels came while we tended our sheep and told us to go find a baby in Bethlehem wrapped in cloths and lying in a manger. And we did. We saw him. The Messiah has come. To God be the glory!"

Every time I read this narrative, it challenges me to imitate the shepherds and make known the message of God who came in human flesh to earth. But to tell the truth, I am not like the shepherds—out front proclaiming to whomever will listen. Rather, I serve those who are out front—I shepherd the shepherds, so to speak. And sometimes I feel guilty about that.

But I do truly want everyone to hear this news. That is why I joined an agency that sends global workers to parts of the world where there is limited access to this message. I support those workers by helping them stay healthy, so they can keep sharing the news of the birth of the Messiah.

Scripture reminds me that my motivation must be love—not guilt that I don't measure up to the shepherds: "For Christ's love compels us, because we are convinced that one died for all, and therefore all died" (2 Corinthians 5:14).

I relate more to Mary in the narrative in Luke 2. She inspires me to ponder and treasure the truth that Jesus came to announce the coming of his new kingdom and sacrifice himself so that all who believe may enter that kingdom. And I sprinkle these musings throughout my teaching and writing.

REFLECTION AND DISCUSSION

In what ways do you share the news of the birth of Jesus?

How can you treasure and ponder the truths of this narrative?

What have you heard and seen that you can praise God for?

PRAYER

Lord God, I confess that I beat myself up for not being an exuberant, verbal storyteller like the shepherds were. May your love compel me to find ways to share that are honoring to you and congruent with my personality and gifts. Keep me pondering and treasuring the magnitude of this message so that it permeates all I do and say.

FURTHER STUDY

Luke 2:8–20

2 Corinthians 5:11–15

TWENTY-TWO

Refugee

*On coming to the house, [Magi from the east] saw
the child with his mother Mary, and they bowed
down and worshiped him. Then they opened their
treasures and presented him with gifts of gold,
frankincense and myrrh.*

Matthew 2:11

When Jesus was born, his mother, Mary, had no gender
reveal party, no baby shower, no birth announcement, no
balloons, no visitors in the waiting room, and no social media
posts. Instead, angels and shepherds proclaimed the news.
Mary and Joseph then stayed in Bethlehem for about one to
two years until the second group of unique visitors arrived—
Magi from the east.

Any sense of safety or normalcy that Mary might have
envisioned for herself and her family evaporated with the
departure of the Magi:

> *When they had gone, an angel of the Lord*
> *appeared to Joseph in a dream. "Get up," he said,*
> *"take the child and his mother and escape to Egypt.*
> *Stay there until I tell you, for Herod is going to*
> *search for the child to kill him." So he got up, took*
> *the child and his mother during the night and left for*
> *Egypt, where he stayed until the death of Herod.*

> *Matthew 2:13–15a*

Thus began Mary's life as a refugee. She fled in the dead of night, lived in a foreign country, learned another language, and possibly experienced prejudice. Imagine too that some of the friends she left behind lost their sons even as she kept hers safe (Matthew 2:16). And just when she'd adjusted to Egypt, she was on the move again:

> *After Herod died, an angel of the Lord appeared in a dream to Joseph in Egypt and said, "Get up, take the child and his mother and go to the land of Israel, for those who were trying to take the child's life are dead." So he got up, took the child and his mother and went to the land of Israel. But when he heard that Archelaus was reigning in Judea in place of his father Herod, he was afraid to go there. Having been warned in a dream, he withdrew to the district of Galilee, and he went and lived in a town called Nazareth. So was fulfilled what was said through the prophets, that he would be called a Nazarene.*
>
> *Matthew 2:19–23*

Mary's life was chaotic, unstable, unsafe. Even after she returned to her home country, she still lived in occupied territory. Refugee. Evacuee. Pierced.

On January 17, 2000, I fled Lombok Island, Indonesia, at two o'clock in the morning on a jet boat with my husband, two young sons, and teammates. We left so we would not find ourselves in the path of Muslim mobs that were systematically destroying homes and churches of Christians throughout the island. I know many have shared similar experiences. Men and women around the globe move constantly, live in occupied territory, and make hard decisions to protect their children from constant danger.

Tucked away in this narrative we find a beautiful statement about Mary that gives us insight into how she could withstand the many soul piercings she endured, including evacuation: "But Mary treasured all these things, pondering them in her heart."

Treasured means "to remember or keep in mind lest it be forgotten" and pondered means "to consider, confer with oneself or dispute mentally."

Mary wrote a mental diary of everything that happened to her so she wouldn't forget, and then she tried to make sense of it by debating within herself. I believe she probably reminded herself again and again what the angel had told her, the identity of her son, the words of Elizabeth, Simeon, and Anna, the miracle of her conception, Joseph's dreams, the amazing visitors, and their glorious gifts that had most likely funded their journeys.

Repeatedly during our evacuation, the words of Proverbs 18:10 came to mind: "The name of the Lord is a fortified tower; the righteous run to it and are safe." In the days following, I recorded everything in my journal. I treasured the ways God had protected us. I poured out my fears. I asked sincere questions. I turned to God's promises in Scripture. All this pondering helped me to make sense of the chaos and find safety.

REFLECTION AND DISCUSSION

How has your life been unsettled, unsafe, and chaotic?

How can you treasure and ponder to make sense of it?

PRAYER

Sovereign God, you are my refuge when I feel like a refugee. You are my strong tower. I run to you and I am safe. Help me remember all you have done for me, and clarify your ways.

FURTHER STUDY

Isaiah 26:4

Matthew 10:28

John 14:27

TWENTY-THREE

Anxious

*Now [Mary and Joseph] went to Jerusalem every year
at the Feast of the Passover. And when [Jesus] was
twelve years old, they went up according to custom. And
when the feast was ended, as they were returning, the
boy Jesus stayed behind in Jerusalem. His parents did
not know it, but supposing him to be in the group they
went a day's journey, but then they began to search for
him among their relatives and acquaintances, and when
they did not find him, they returned to Jerusalem,
searching for him. After three days they found him in
the temple, sitting among the teachers, listening to them
and asking them questions. And all who heard him
were amazed at his understanding and his answers.
And when his parents saw him, they were astonished.
And his mother said to him, "Son, why have you
treated us so? Behold, your father and I have been
searching for you in great distress." And he said to
them, "Why were you looking for me? Did you not
know that I must be in my Father's house?" And they
did not understand the saying that he spoke to them.
And he went down with them and came to Nazareth
and was submissive to them. And his mother treasured
up all these things in her heart. And Jesus increased in
wisdom and in stature and in favor with God and man.*

Luke 2:41–52 (ESV)

I can relate to Mary's anxiety. We lost our five-year-old son in
Heathrow airport. One minute we all sat waiting at the gate,
the next, he was gone. I did not see him wander off. I looked

up and he had simply disappeared. A very panicked ten minutes ensued as we searched up and down the walkways for a small, blond boy. When we found him a few aisles over, the anger in our voices surprised him, for he had been exploring out of curiosity. Ten minutes felt like eternity. I cannot imagine three days of searching.

In our security-conscious society, we struggle to believe a parent would not notice a child's absence. But in Mary's day, hundreds of Jewish pilgrims traveled home together after celebrating the Passover in Jerusalem. Men and women walked separately while the children ran back and forth between groups, playing and enjoying the company of cousins and friends. At the end of the day, Mary and Joseph met up to settle down for the night. I can imagine the conversation.

"Where's Jesus? I thought he was with you."

"No, wasn't he with you?" Distressed. Anxious. Pierced.

Jesus could not be found, and so they retraced their steps to Jerusalem. Three days later—thirty-six hours without 911 or missing persons posters or a Nazareth Facebook group—they found him in the temple answering questions from the religious leaders. Astonished and amazed, they blurted out, "Son, why have you done this to us? We have been anxiously searching for you."

Mary used a word that means "to cause intense pain, to be in anguish or tormented." When I finally found my son in Heathrow, I too blurted out angry words, blaming him for causing me distress. Fear often expresses itself that way.

Jesus essentially responded, "What? Why so worried? Chill. I am right where I should be. I am in my Father's house doing his business. I know what I'm doing."

Now add confusion to anxiety. So, how did Mary respond? Once again, she "treasured all these things in her heart." In this instance, treasured means "to keep continually or carefully." Mary stored this experience away in her heart, putting it together with the promises of the angel: "he will save his people from their sins" (Matthew 1:21); "he will be great" (Luke 1:32); "he will reign" (Luke 1:33). Seeing that Jesus was not lost but doing exactly what he had come for calmed her fears.

REFLECTION AND DISCUSSION

What are you anxious about today? Especially regarding your children or your mentees?

What business is your Father about that might comfort your anxious heart?

What promises from God do you need to treasure today?

PRAYER

Jesus, thank you that you constantly do your Father's business. I resolve to treasure your promises and remember that you remain exactly where you should be. As I do this, please take away my anxiety.

FURTHER STUDY

Matthew 6:34

John 6:38–40

Romans 8:38–39

TWENTY-FOUR

Treasure and Ponder

*But Mary treasured up all these things and pondered
them in her heart.*

Luke 2:19

But his mother treasured all these things in her heart.

Luke 2:51b

Netflix has produced yet another version of the classic Anne of Green Gables story called *Anne with an E*. In this series, Anne's adopted mother, Marilla, opens her closet, reaches high up on a shelf behind other things and pulls out an old box. She lovingly opens it to reveal a bundle of old love letters tied up with a bow. Then she sits down in a rocker and slowly opens a letter, remembering the love of a former beau.[21] Marilla depicts what we often do with items of sentimental value that we want to keep and treasure.

Mary's heart was pierced over and over. Yet she managed to remain a faithful disciple of her son. So that we too can live with and survive a pierced heart, Mary gave us a beautiful practice we can imitate. In Luke 2:19, treasured (*syntereo*) means "to remember or keep in mind lest it be forgotten." This is the same word that Luke uses in 5:38 "But new wine must be put into new wineskins, and both are *preserved*" (emphasis mine, NKJV).

Pondered (*symballo*) means "to consider, dispute mentally, or reflect." In Acts 4:15, this word is translated *conferred*: "So they ordered them to withdraw from the Sanhedrin and then conferred together."

The Luke 2:51 passage uses a different Greek word for treasured (*diatereo*). Here it means "to keep continually," as in 1 Timothy 3:9: "They must *keep hold* of the deep truths of the faith" (emphasis mine).

Mary kept a mental treasure box of everything that happened to her so she wouldn't forget. Then she tried to make sense of it by debating within herself and reflecting often.

To illustrate what this means for us today, let me bring Mary into the 21st century. If Mary were alive today, I think she would make a scrapbook or find a keepsake box for her "love letters from God."

First, she would remember. "Remember" is the second most common command in the Bible after "fear not." In her box she might put (in either object or word form) the sayings of the angel, Joseph, shepherds, Elizabeth, Simeon, and even Jesus himself. This way she could remind herself again of the promises, the miracles, the dreams, the amazing visitors, and the fulfilled prophecies.

Then she would reflect. As Mary might touch each item in her box and take them out, she would consider what it all meant—the words, the miracles, the promises, the pain. She would wrestle in her soul and debate with herself in order to understand it all.

And finally, she would retain. Mary might keep everything to refer to in the future, to give her comfort and faith when the next piercing came along.

I have my own set of love letters from the Lord in my treasure box. I don't keep a physical box, but I have these truths on cards and bookmarks and magnets and in the notes on my smart phone.

As we grow older, perhaps the practice of pondering and treasuring becomes even more vital. With each passing year, we see more and more evil and disappointment. When the realities of life don't mesh with our current understanding of God, we are susceptible to disillusionment, cynicism, and doubt. Someone I love very much has made the decision to leave the truths they followed for fifty years and move away from God. This has reminded me we cannot trust that age and experience alone are adequate to withstand our piercings. Instead, we must continue to remember, reflect, and retain.

REFLECTION AND DISCUSSION

How can you treasure and ponder? (Suggestions include a box of remembrance, a collection of objects, a special file on your computer, a scrapbook.)

What first step will you take today to begin this practice?

PRAYER

Savior God, how quickly I forget. When life confuses me and I don't understand my circumstances, help me to remember your promises, your marvelous deeds, and your incredible plan for me.

FURTHER STUDY

Psalm 77:11

Luke 8:15

2 Timothy 2:7

TWENTY-FIVE

Widow

The Lord God said, "It is not good for the man to be alone. I will make a helper suitable for him."

Genesis 2:18

God blessed [Adam and Eve] and said to them, "Be fruitful and increase in number; fill the earth and subdue it. Rule over the fish in the sea and the birds in the sky and over every living creature that moves on the ground."

Genesis 1:28

I have a beautiful Italian Fontanini nativity set. Year after year I had set it up not really knowing which figure was Joseph. I finally searched Google and discovered that I do actually have Joseph. He just looks like another shepherd! Once again, I noticed how often authors, artists, and preachers sideline Joseph in the story of Jesus's birth.

However, Joseph—the unsung hero—deserves much applause in Mary's story. In fact, he was indispensable in helping her fulfill her commission. While he did not play a direct role in Jesus's conception, his bloodline was vitally important. For Mary's son to be the legitimate Messiah in the eyes of the Jews, his father had to be of the lineage of King David (Luke 2:4). God sovereignly ensured this in two ways: his mother, Mary, descended from David through his son Nathan, and his father, Joseph, through another son,

Solomon. While not Jesus's father by blood, Joseph was his legal father.

Joseph's heritage was important, not just because of his famous ancestor, but more so because it meant he was a "seed bearer." Ever since the sin of Adam and Eve destroyed God's perfect world, God had been carefully preparing to restore order by sending the seed, or offspring, of the woman to crush Satan's head (Genesis 3:15). Each male that God appointed as the firstborn heir carried the seed from that point on all the way up to Joseph of Nazareth, the carpenter.

While Mary also descended from King David, her lineage wasn't the point here. After all, we find non-Jewish women—Tamar, Rahab, and Ruth—who also bore the seed. The father's bloodline determined the seed.

What a husband God provided for Mary. A kind man who did not want Mary to endure disgrace. A righteous man who chose to act honorably despite the norms of his shame-based culture (Matthew 1:19). An obedient man who without hesitation followed God's order to marry his pregnant fiancée and accept the child as his own (Matthew 1:20).

Mary and Joseph beautifully illustrate what one of my favorite authors has coined the "blessed alliance." Carolyn Custis James uses this phrase to describe God's plan from the beginning that men and women work together to build his kingdom. Of Joseph she says:

> He shuts down his carpenter shop, gets behind his wife's calling, and adapts himself to his wife and God's calling on her life. His whole life will be committed to making sure she succeeds in carrying out the mission God has entrusted to her.[22]

Even though Joseph accomplished the powerful mission of the blessed alliance he was called to in his lifetime, he died before Jesus began his public ministry.[23] Mary became a widow. Pierced.

In Mary's culture, the oldest son would bear the responsibility of taking care of a widowed mother. Jesus, however, was wandering around the countryside with no income.

Since tradition says that Mary moved to Capernaum with Jesus when he began his public ministry, perhaps the women who traveled with the disciples included Mary in their financial support of Jesus (Luke 8:1–3), or perhaps Mary's other children took on the responsibility—we do not know. (But we do know from John 19:25–27 that Jesus intentionally and tenderly made sure that Mary was taken care of after his death.) All things considered, Mary must have acutely felt the loss of her biggest supporter, ally, and partner, Joseph.

When my best friend died after a ten-year battle with cancer, her husband became a widower. His soul was deeply pierced. He lost the other half of his alliance, his counterpart. I witnessed the huge adjustment he endured in an effort to navigate life without a partner by his side, especially one deeply committed to serving God together.

Scripture doesn't tell us how Mary coped. But I believe her faith and her ability to ponder things in her heart helped her through this. She always kept her focus on her commission and got personally involved in Jesus's mission, even encouraging him to begin his public ministry (John 2:1–5).

Fortunately, blessed alliances are not just for husbands and wives. Mary had the ongoing opportunity to partner in ministry with her brothers, the disciples. May we too, whether we have an earthly spouse or not, stay focused on building God's kingdom, and may we form many blessed alliances with our brothers and sisters.

REFLECTION AND DISCUSSION

In what instances have you experienced a "blessed alliance"?

Have you ever lost a dear partner (spouse, ministry, or accountability etc.)? How is Jesus providing for you?

How can you get involved in Jesus's mission?

PRAYER

Lord God, our provider, thank you for the beautiful example of Joseph who adapted his life to ensure that Mary could fulfill the calling you gave her. Give us more men like Joseph. And when we are separated from precious partners, keep us committed to seeing your kingdom come.

FURTHER STUDY

Genesis 3:15

Matthew 1:1–16

Romans 16:1–15

TWENTY-SIX

Letting Go

*On the third day a wedding took place at Cana in
Galilee. Jesus' mother was there, and Jesus and his
disciples had also been invited to the wedding. When the
wine was gone, Jesus' mother said to him, "They have no
more wine." "Woman, why do you involve me?" Jesus
replied. "My hour has not yet come." His mother said
to the servants, "Do whatever he tells you."*

John 2:1–5

Mary's son, Jesus—the Messiah—had yet to reveal himself to
the world. She had kept his mission in her heart and
pondered it for three decades. Now the opportunity had
come. Finally, he could show his power.

But Jesus responded in a startling way. He called Mary
"woman." Not mother, mummy, mama, mom, or the
Aramaic equivalent. This, from her dearly loved son that she
had carried, birthed, and raised. What did he mean by this?

Jesus's choice of word told his mother their relationship
would be different from now on. No longer under her
authority, he would act only at the initiative of his Father.
Once again, Jesus reminded Mary that he would be about his
Father's business, on God's timetable. She had to refrain
from interfering and let him make his own choices.

Even if Mary totally understood that Jesus meant no
disrespect and still loved her very much, there had to be

some pang, however small. There is always loss and grief when a parent realizes that things have changed in their relationship with their child. Letting go. Pierced.

My young adult sons no longer live under my roof. I have to let them go. During our family vacation last summer, I took a solitary walk on the beach. I needed to think, to pray, to ask God to help me release my son to the next chapter in his life —a committed relationship and potential wife. Grieving the fact that this change meant limited individual time with him and trying not to have a pity party because the dynamics had changed, I really wanted to be mature and do this well.

Then I looked up and saw him jogging down the beach, coming my way. And he saw me. My heart leapt! For one irrational moment, I thought, *he's coming to talk to me and walk with me*; then he waved, called out, "Hi mom," and jogged on by.

I laughed out loud. What was I thinking?

What has helped me release my sons is an experiential understanding of God's merciful love for me. This love is described in Isaiah 54:10:

> "For the mountains shall depart
> And the hills be removed,
> But My kindness shall not depart from you,
> Nor shall My covenant of peace be removed,"
> Says the Lord, who has mercy on you." (NKJV)

I believe Mary could let Jesus go to fulfill his mission because she too understood this love as expressed in her words in Luke 1:50: "His mercy extends to those who fear him."

The Hebrew word for mercy—*racham*—sometimes translated as compassion, means a love like that of a parent for a child, especially an infant. Knowing that God had a tender, heartfelt concern for her would certainly have helped Mary as it has done for me.

While we rear our children to become independent of us, God raises us to become more and more dependent on him. He never lets us go.

REFLECTION AND DISCUSSION

In what ways do you struggle with letting your children (or spiritual children) go?

Has someone that you have mentored and discipled surpassed you? Are you still trying to keep them under your wing? How can you encourage them to be about their Father's business?

PRAYER

Merciful Father, I rejoice that you will never let me go, nor will you ever let my children go. Thank you that because of your compassionate love, I can take the step of faith to let them go to serve you and fulfill their calling, just as Mary released Jesus to complete his mission of saving the world.

FURTHER STUDY

Psalm 103:13

Isaiah 49:15

John 3:28–30

TWENTY-SEVEN

Grieved

*Jesus left there and went to his hometown, accompanied
by his disciples. When the Sabbath came, he began to
teach in the synagogue, and many who heard him were
amazed. "Where did this man get these things?" they
asked. "What's this wisdom that has been given him?
What are these remarkable miracles he is performing?
Isn't this the carpenter? Isn't this Mary's son and the
brother of James, Joseph, Judas and Simon? Aren't his
sisters here with us?" And they took offense at him.*

Mark 6:1–3

When we returned from the mission field, we put our sons in
a private Christian school. We thought the environment
would be less of a shock to our missionary kids, but that
proved not to be the case. How I struggled to watch them
adjust to a new culture, make friends, understand idioms, wait
for invitations, and figure out their new life. I grieved for my
boys. I wanted to take away their hurt and pain. I wanted
them to be happy.

How much more so, Mary grieved for her son. Listen to
what Mary had to witness and endure on his behalf:

Among the crowds there was widespread whispering
about him. Some said, "He is a good man." Others
replied, "No, he deceives the people." (John 7:12)

"You are demon-possessed," the crowd answered. (John 7:20)

All the people in the synagogue were furious when they heard this. They got up, drove [Jesus] out of the town, and took him to the brow of the hill on which the town was built, in order to throw him off the cliff. (Luke 4:28–29)

They were using this question as a trap, in order to have a basis for accusing him. (John 8:6a)

Then the Pharisees went out and began to plot with the Herodians how they might kill Jesus. (Mark 3:6)

The chief priests and the whole Sanhedrin were looking for evidence against Jesus so that they could put him to death, but they did not find any. Many testified falsely against him, but their statements did not agree. (Mark 14:55–56)

Grieved. Hurt. Pierced. Surely Mary felt the pain of Jesus's rejection by the community and loss of reputation among the neighbors. Usually celebrities have total acceptance and carte blanche among the home crowd. When they don't, it pierces even more.

No mother wants her child to be an offense to others. We want our children, grandchildren, nieces, nephews, and those we mentor to be liked, accepted, respected, and loved by all. And how much more grieved are mothers of children with disabilities or social anxieties or mental illness? These moms especially understand the words of the author of Hebrews: "Continue to remember those in prison as if you were together with them in prison, and those who are mistreated as if you yourselves were suffering" (Hebrews 13:3).

How did Mary respond? Did she rankle at the injustice? Was she angry at the mockers? Was she tempted to speak up in his defense? Or did she wish he wouldn't be so bold or abrasive? Maybe change his tone or his approach?

Why does he say such controversial things? Why did he do that? Doesn't he realize the neighbors are talking? I don't want him to get hurt. Play it safe so that he doesn't have to suffer. Be normal so nobody notices. Had she expected that the Savior would be embraced with open arms? Did she think he could take David's throne peacefully?

I think Mary did what she had always done. She remembered the prophecies, the exact words of the angel, Jesus's reply in the temple. And she pondered. The miracles he performed showed his power over death, illness, and nature. The words he spoke revealed his identity as the Bread of Life, the Lamb of God, the Door, the Way, the Light, the Living Water.

I believe Mary's unwavering faith enabled her to stand with Jesus in his pain and support him with her presence. And eventually, her journey led her to become a true disciple, to actively participate in the first church planting effort—to deliver the gospel as she had delivered the One who is the Good News.

REFLECTION AND DISCUSSION

What words and actions have you witnessed about your loved ones that have pierced your soul?

How can you channel your grieving into spreading the gospel?

PRAYER

Lord Jesus, I pray for all who grieve watching their children struggle to lead a normal life, to be accepted and loved. I pray for those whose hearts are pierced because of the pain their loved ones endure due to the ignorance and cruelty of others. Strengthen their faith, remind them that you too endured ridicule and rejection, and show them how to transform their pain into spreading the news of your salvation.

FURTHER STUDY

Deuteronomy 10:17–18

Isaiah 49:13

2 Corinthians 1:3–4

Parent of Unbelievers

*Jesus' brothers said to him, "Leave Galilee and go
to Judea, so that your disciples there may see the
works you do. No one who wants to become a public
figure acts in secret. Since you are doing these things,
show yourself to the world." For even his own
brothers did not believe in him.*

John 7:3–5

*Then Jesus entered a house, and again a crowd
gathered, so that he and his disciples were not even
able to eat. When his family heard about this, they
went to take charge of him, for they said, "He is
out of his mind."*

Mark 3:20–21

The Gospel of Mark tells us that Mary had other children—
James, Joseph, Judas (Jude), Simeon, and at least two
daughters (Mark 6:3). One can only speculate about life with
Jesus as an older brother. But Scripture does give us a few
glimpses into their relationship.

Jesus's brothers did not believe in him. Thinking him crazy,
they tried to take charge of him and shut him down. Perhaps
they couldn't get past the fact that he forfeited his
responsibilities around the home. Perhaps his perfection
convicted them. Perhaps they resented his popularity.
Perhaps they hated being pushed into the spotlight to answer

questions about him. After all, to them he was just Jesus, their big brother.

What strain this must have put on Mary's relationship with them. How hard it must have been to have children who didn't believe, even after all the years of recounting the angel's visit, promises, the escape to Egypt, and the miracles.

A parent of unbelievers. Pierced. Mary knew the pain of a mother whose children do not follow the Savior, even though they have heard the gospel and seen the handiwork of God since infancy. Any mother is torn when her children don't get along or have each other's back. Mary balanced the delicate tightrope of supporting Jesus's mission and loving all her children.

Thankfully, Mary's pain didn't last forever. Somewhere along the way, her sons began to hear, listen, and believe the truth about their unique brother. After the resurrection, Jesus appeared to her son James (1 Corinthians 15:7), and all the brothers joined together in constant prayer with the new church (Acts 1:14). James then became a leader of the congregation in Jerusalem (Acts 15:13–22, Galatians 2:9) and wrote the epistle of James, according to most scholars. Mary's other son Judas also wrote an epistle (Jude), and her sons and their wives took missionary journeys (1 Corinthians 9:5). I think we can safely assume that Mary's stalwart faith and belief in her son Jesus eventually helped her other children to also believe.

Many of my dear friends have children who don't believe. I often sit and pray with them as tears and sorrow overtake. They wonder what they did wrong. They blame themselves. They long for their children to love and follow Jesus.

The apostle John says: "No one who is born of God will continue to sin, because God's seed remains in them; they cannot go on sinning, because they have been born of

God" (1 John 3:9). May this be a comfort to all parents and spiritual mentors. If the seeds of faith and salvation are in your children, remember that their journey has only begun. The Holy Spirit is always wooing a wayward child or a skeptic (Jeremiah 31:3).

A friend who walks this same road as Mary told me, "This is something I must daily surrender to God and trust that he will be just and good with the outcome, with how the story ends."

REFLECTION AND DISCUSSION

In what ways are you a parent of unbelievers?

How does Mary's example encourage you today?

PRAYER

Jesus, thank you that the example of a godly mother can influence an unbelieving child. I pray for my friends who know the piercing of this pain. Please help them to have stalwart faith and unwavering belief in you and your Spirit to draw back their children. May your goodness and justice bring them hope.

FURTHER STUDY

Luke 19:10

John 12:32

Philippians 1:6

2 Peter 3:9

TWENTY-NINE

Redefined

*Then Jesus entered a house, and again a crowd gathered,
so that he and his disciples were not even able to eat.
When his family heard about this, they went to take
charge of him, for they said, "He is out of his mind."
… Then Jesus' mother and brothers arrived. Standing
outside, they sent someone in to call him. A crowd was
sitting around him, and they told him, "Your mother
and brothers are outside looking for you." "Who are my
mother and my brothers?" he asked. Then he looked at
those seated in a circle around him and said, "Here are
my mother and my brothers! Whoever does God's will is
my brother and sister and mother."*
Mark 3:20–21, 31–35

About two full years into his ministry and followed by large crowds, Jesus garnered great controversy. His family heard the reports and thought him crazy. Since "take charge of" means "to take custody of," they must have intended to take Jesus away, probably back home. This family intervention intended to rein in their out-of-his-mind brother.

But Jesus did not acknowledge Mary and her other sons as his family. "These others are my mother." Ouch. It must have hurt to hear these words after all she had done. At first glance, this doesn't sound like the words of a dedicated son. They could sting, unless one looks at the true meaning behind them. Redefined. Pierced.

Scholars disagree on Mary's motive behind this intervention. Some think she sided with Jesus's brothers. For her to take this step, she must have felt he had gone too far and needed a cautioning mother talk.

However, Dr. Timothy Ralston of Dallas Theological Seminary feels that this doesn't fit with the Mary we see in Scripture. The word translated as out of his mind "describes someone who is confused or has lost something, including one's spiritual and/or mental balance, one's path, or something else. This 'loss of way' can be described as 'becoming distracted or diverted' ... Mary's concern is that the excessive demands of the crowd have distracted and diverted Jesus from his larger Messianic responsibilities. Her son, she believes, is in danger of losing his way."[24]

While we can neither attribute a flawless faith to Mary nor assign motive to her actions, we do know that she had to learn that Jesus's mission, and his way of fulfilling it did not look like what she envisioned. In his usual manner of turning things upside down, he did it here by redefining his family. Of course, Jesus didn't hate his family nor want to cut them out of his life. He simply described his true family members as those in the kingdom of God, those who do God's will.

Joseph H. Hellerman writes that in Jesus's world, blood relationships trumped all others, with the brother-sister bond being the strongest. Because marriages were arranged for the continuance of the patrilineal line and brides were strangers in their new home, primary affection and loyalty belonged to one's siblings. Therefore, when Jesus said that one's spiritual brothers and sisters took precedence over one's blood siblings, he upended the cultural norm.[25]

Jesus reiterated this new spiritual relationship again in Matthew 10:37: "Anyone who loves their father or mother more than me is not worthy of me; anyone who loves their son or daughter more than me is not worthy of me." Mary, like all disciples, had to be in a faith relationship with Jesus and follow his agenda. Carolyn Custis James explains it this way:

> Physically giving birth to Jesus ultimately meant nothing if Mary never listened, believed, and lived out the teachings of her son. Her true calling in life —and the only bond with him that endures—was to hear his words and to live by them. Her greatest calling was to follow Jesus and cultivate the family resemblance by becoming like her son.[26]

Life on a missionary team taught me to redefine family. Teammates became brothers and sisters, aunts and uncles, and even grandparents. We frequented each other's homes for meals, game and movie nights, holidays, and celebrations. We played together, laughed together, and cried together. This concept of familial relationships established through Jesus's blood brings comfort to the unmarried, the widow, the childless, and the orphan, as it must have to Mary when Jesus was no longer with her on earth.

REFLECTION AND DISCUSSION

Compare the emphasis you put on your blood relationships to that of your spiritual family.

How might you have idolized your nuclear family to the point of excluding others?

PRAYER

Father God, teach us what it means to be the family of God, to show our connection by doing your will and loving you most of all. Teach us how to prioritize our spiritual relationships. Help us invite and include our spiritual siblings in our homes.

FURTHER STUDY

1 Corinthians 12:12–27

Galatians 6:10

1 Timothy 5:1–2

THIRTY

Torn

Carrying his own cross, [Jesus] went out to the place of the Skull (which in Aramaic is called Golgotha). There they crucified him, and with him two others—one on each side and Jesus in the middle. Pilate had a notice prepared and fastened to the cross. It read: JESUS OF NAZARETH, THE KING OF THE JEWS ... Near the cross of Jesus stood his mother, his mother's sister, Mary the wife of Clopas, and Mary Magdalene. When Jesus saw his mother there, and the disciple whom he loved standing nearby, he said to her, "Woman, here is your son," and to the disciple, "Here is your mother." From that time on, this disciple took her into his home.

John 19:17–19, 25–27

As the future of her precious son grew bleaker, Mary waited nearby, speculating, praying, crying, anxious for any news. I imagine she knew of (if not even witnessed) his betrayal by a friend, the mockery of a trial, the false accusations, and the severe beating. I think she probably followed as he staggered to carry his cross (Luke 23:27), felt every horrifying hammer pound, and shivered with each agonizing breath. She heard the insults hurled at him, watched the soldiers gamble for his cloak and taunt him (John 19:25). And she gazed on him as he cried out his final words and gasped for his last breath.

How she must have hurt along with him. How she must have wanted to make the pain stop, hold him in her arms, tell him it would be all right. Did she doubt? Did she wonder if she heard the angel correctly? In all her remembering and pondering, did she imagine this? Was this really the way of salvation? Where was the crown, the throne, the scepter? When would these awful Romans be overthrown? Torn. Pierced.

Studies show that the pain of losing a child is one of the most severe. My counselor husband tells me that this trauma is "brain altering" because of what it does chemically on a cellular level. This particular pain—the death of a child—has resulted in forsaken faith, broken marriages, and joyless lives. A friend who just lost her young adult son signs her posts as "a broken mother."

I don't claim to understand the piercing involved in holding children, raising them, and then having them torn from your arms. I can only mourn with my friends who do. But loss comes in other forms as well. I have experienced the piercing of miscarriage and the death of ministry partners, friends, and parents.

When no other siblings followed Jesus and all male disciples, except John, had turned and run, Mary (and her sister) stayed faithfully by the cross. Even though God the Father needed to forsake him in order to save us (Matthew 27:46), Mary did not. She could not alleviate his suffering, but she could comfort with her presence.

Even as Mary experienced the piercing of her soul, Jesus was pierced for her. As her soul was wounded, his wounds paid the price for her soul. As Mary's presence comforted her son, his provision for a new family comforted her (John 19:25–27). As her heart broke for her son, so his heart broke for her.

Jesus knew the pain of his mother's piercings. And he understands our pain and our piercings. He was pierced for you and me as well.

But he was pierced for our transgressions, he was crushed for our iniquities; the punishment that brought us peace was on him, and by his wounds we are healed. (Isaiah 53:5)

Because he himself suffered when he was tempted, he is able to help those who are being tempted. (Hebrews 2:18)

REFLECTION AND DISCUSSION

How can you relate to Mary in the loss of her son?

How has Jesus's suffering alleviated yours?

PRAYER

Jesus, our sacrificed Lamb, thank you for suffering and being pierced for us. You died that Mary might be saved. You were pierced for my sins. Your wounds have healed me. Thank you that Mary found salvation through your piercings.

Isaiah 53:3–8

2 Corinthians 12:9–10

THIRTY-ONE

Healed

*On the first day of the week, very early in the morning,
the women took the spices they had prepared and went
to the tomb. They found the stone rolled away from the
tomb, but when they entered, they did not find the body
of the Lord Jesus. While they were wondering about
this, suddenly two men in clothes that gleamed like
lightning stood beside them. In their fright the women
bowed down with their faces to the ground, but the men
said to them, "Why do you look for the living among the
dead? He is not here; he has risen! Remember how he
told you, while he was still with you in Galilee: 'The
Son of Man must be delivered over to the hands of
sinners, be crucified and on the third day be raised
again.'" Then they remembered his words.*

Luke 24:1–8

No record exists of Jesus showing himself specifically to
Mary after his resurrection, but since "he presented himself
to [the disciples] and gave many convincing proofs that he
was alive" (Acts 1:3), I have no doubt that Mary saw her son
in the flesh again.

Perhaps she ran to the tomb in the wee hours of the
morning with the other women to tend to Jesus's body.
Perhaps she remained with John because he had assumed the
responsibility to care for her. We don't know if she had
private words with Jesus, but what we do know is enough.

Her son was alive. God had fulfilled the promise given to her by the angel. Her treasured memories and pondered thoughts finally began to make sense. The one born to save his people from their sins saved her, his own mother. What joy. Her soul that had been pierced over and over was now healed by her son's piercing—her Savior.

As Mary gave birth to and supported Jesus through his whole life and death, she helped give birth to and support the new church (Acts 1:14) after witnessing the power of the resurrection. Tradition suggests she lived with John, serving the church in Ephesus until her death.[27]

Mary was the favored one. Because of God's grace alone, he chose her to bring the Savior into the world and raise him.

Mary was the blessed one. She surrendered to God's will from the start and believed that what he said would come to pass. God blessed her when she obeyed and became a member of his kingdom.

Mary was the pierced one. She felt every prick of anxiety, rejection, and pain associated with her son's unique mission. And as a result, she found the joy of salvation.

With grace came blessing and pain and healing. Mary endured and demonstrated to us how to be a disciple—surrender, believe, treasure, and ponder.

Like Mary, we too are favored, blessed, and pierced. We can say with Mary, "My soul glorifies the Lord and my spirit rejoices in God my Savior, for he has been mindful of the humble state of his servant" (Luke 1:46–48).

REFLECTION AND DISCUSSION

How does knowing that Jesus was pierced for you bring you healing?

In what ways do you most relate to Mary and why?

What aspects of Mary's example of a disciple can you apply to your own life?

PRAYER

Savior God, thank you for demonstrating your power over evil and death in your resurrection. Thank you that your wounds healed Mary and that they heal me. Give me your power to testify of this to the world and to become a true disciple like Mary.

FURTHER STUDY

Isaiah 53:5, 9–12

John 20:31

Conclusion

My brothers and sisters,

Follow Mary's example.

Offer yourself as God's servant. Accept his will even when it includes pain. Believe his Word. Worship. Praise. Know the Scriptures. Know Jesus. Know your identity. Obey him. Discover your part in Jesus's mission. Lean on your true family. Let God be about his business. Become a true disciple. Be grateful. Treasure and ponder. Participate in Christ's suffering. Spread the good news. Build the kingdom.

Mary didn't offer a new strategy. The principles of Scripture remain the same. We just need reminders to apply them over and over again in each new circumstance, in deeper ways.

Do them over and over as Mary did.

Thank you for journeying with me through the life of Mary of Nazareth. I have loved sharing her with you. I hope and pray that Mary will remind you that while your soul may be pierced, you are favored and blessed.

More On Mary

Glahn, Sandra, ed. 2017. *Vindicating the Vixens: Revisiting Sexualized, Vilified, and Marginalized Women of the Bible*. Grand Rapids, MI: Kregel Publications. (See chapter 5, "The Virgin Mary," by Dr. Timothy Ralston.)

Hunsader, Joceyln and Alexander Trumpower. 2018. *Mary: A 5 Week Devotional*. Independently published. www.Jocelynhunsader.com/.

James, Carolyn Custis. 2010. *Half the Church: Recapturing God's Global Vision for Women*. Grand Rapids, MI: Zondervan. (See chapter 7, "The Blessed Alliance.")

James, Carolyn Custis. 2005. *Lost Women of the Bible: The Women We Thought We Knew*. Grand Rapids, MI: Zondervan. (See chapter 8, "The First Disciple—Mary of Nazareth.")

James, Carolyn Custis. 2005. *Malestrom: Manhood Swept Into the Currents of a Changing World*. Grand Rapids, MI: Zondervan. (See chapter 7, "Gender Role Reversal.")

Kiker, Mindy and Jenny Kochert. 2018. *Steadfast: Cultivating a Heart Like Mary. A Flourish Bible Study Journal*. Independently published. www.flourishgathering.com/.

Kraft, Vicki. July 16, 2007. *Lesson 10: Mary, Most Blessed of Women*. www.bible.org/seriespage/lesson-10-mary-most-blessed-women/.

McKnight, Scot. 2007. *The Real Mary: Why Evangelical Christians Can Embrace the Mother of Jesus*. Brewster, MA: Paraclete Press.

Pickett, Todd. November 29, 2010. "The Advent of Jesus." Biola University Chapel. www.youtube.com/watch?v=9wt6nTFr3CM&t=455s/.

Roese, Jackie. 2018. *I'm Enough; Learning to Live Confidently in Your Own Skin.* Addison, TX: HIS Publishing Group. (See chapter 7, "She for She Community.")

Roese, Jackie. April 10, 2017. *Living the Blessed Life.* www.JackieAlwaysUplugged.com. www.jackiealwaysunplugged.com/2017/04/10/living-the-blessed-life/.

Leader's Guide

TIPS FOR FACILITATORS

I love to study the Bible. I also love to be part of a study group that is well led. My own journey with studying and leading began as a teenager when my mother gave me a discipleship guide from The Navigators. The process went like this: read scripture, answer the question, fill in the blank. Following that, I taught the middle school girls' Sunday school: tell the Bible story, ask questions, hope they learn the truth.

In college, I discovered the inductive study method through the ministry of InterVarsity Christian Fellowship. I attended their small group leaders' training and began leading peer small groups: observation question, interpretation question, application.

During graduate school for my Christian Education degree, I learned to create a Bible curriculum using: hook, book, look, took.

As a young mom on the mission field, I took all this knowledge and crafted many Sunday school lessons for the children on our team: tell the Bible story, explain it, ask a few questions, sing a song, do a craft, make an application, pray for understanding and transformation.

Then I joined a church staff and began writing and leading women's Bible studies: read the passage, fill in the blanks, pray, make sure every question is answered in class, be the expert.

Next, I attended a year-long class on spiritual practices and discovered spiritual formation groups. Everything changed.

No longer was I responsible to disseminate all the right information. Each group member came prepared. For their allotted time, they shared whatever they desired in relation to the material studied. The rest of the group only listened. No cross talk. No advice giving. No comparison with one's own story. No evaluation of their words. Only affirmation and prayer.

Most recently, I attended a weeklong peer learning workshop. This training built on all of my previous experience. Group members come prepared, having read or studied the preassigned material. The facilitator gives a brief introduction and summary of the topic. He/she asks a good open-ended conversation starter. Discussion flows naturally, only interspersed with more questions to keep it going. I began to take a back seat and let the group teach each other.

In summary, I have learned that typically group leaders and facilitators talk too much. We feel the need to give a commentary every time a group member shares an opinion or answer. We are overly concerned with making sure the "truth" is disseminated, rather than allowing the members to extrapolate that information themselves and the Holy Spirit to be the true teacher.

While *Favored, Blessed, Pierced* is written primarily to be a personal devotional, any study is enriched when we learn in community with others. The experience and insight of others can only challenge and expand our perception and application of Mary's example.

So, whether you use one of the following suggested formats or create your own, let me encourage you to moderate your verbal space; don't try to fix others or give advice; listen without interruption or judgment and let the discussion flow. True learning that leads to life transformation will take place.

SUGGESTED FORMATS

Four-Week Discussion Small Group

Week 1: Favored

- Pre-read entries 1–8.
- Open with prayer and a time of silent reflection.
- Read aloud Luke 1:26–38. (Not only do we talk too much, we read too fast. Slow down when reading Scripture so that the group members can fully hear and absorb the words. Read with expression and thoughtfulness.)
- Ask the following questions, allowing for the discussion to proceed naturally and organically, using peer learning techniques:
    - *What surprised you about Mary's story?*
    - *How can you respond to God's commissioning as Mary did?*
- Read the verses for further study.
- Ask: *How do these passages add to your understanding of Mary's story and example?*
- Conclude with prayer.

Week 2: Blessed

- Pre-read entries 9–16.
- Open with prayer and a time of silent reflection.
- Read (slowly and thoughtfully) Luke 1:39–55; Matthew 5:3–11; Luke 11:27–28.
- Ask the following questions, allowing for the discussion to proceed naturally and organically using peer learning techniques:
  - *What surprised you about Mary's story?*
  - *How are you blessed according to the biblical meaning of* makarios*?*
- Read the verses for further study.
- Ask: *How do these passages add to your understanding of Mary's story and example?*
- Conclude with prayer.

Week 3: Pierced

- Pre-read entries 17–24.
- Open with prayer and a time of silent reflection.
- Choose some of the references to read (slowly and thoughtfully).
- Ask the following questions, allowing for the discussion to proceed naturally and organically using peer learning techniques:
  - *What surprised you about Mary's story?*
  - *In what way do you relate to Mary's piercings?*
- How can you begin to ponder and treasure today?
- Read the verses for further study.
- Ask: *How do these passages add to your understanding of Mary's story and example?*
- Conclude with prayer.

Week 4: Healed

- Pre-read entries 25–31 and Conclusion.
- Open with prayer and a time of silent reflection.
- Read aloud (slowly and thoughtfully) John 19:17–19, 25–27; Luke 24:1–8.
- Ask the following questions, allowing for the discussion to proceed naturally and organically using peer learning techniques:
    - *What surprised you about Mary's story?*
    - *In what way do you relate to Mary's piercings?*
    - *How have Jesus's piercings healed you?*
- Read the verses for further study.
- Ask: *How do these passages add to your understanding of Mary's story and example?*
- Conclude with prayer.

One-time Spiritual Formation Gathering

- Ask group members to read all of the entries prior to the meeting.

- Decide how long each group member can speak by dividing up the time by the number of attendees.

- Give each member uninterrupted time to tell the group whatever they desire about their takeaway from the reading. If they need a prompt, they can share what surprised and challenged them about the life of Mary.

- If time remains after all have shared, go around again to allow for members to affirm statements and comments made in the first round. Be sure to leave time for prayer.

Notes

1 Rev. Dr. David Handy, e-mail message to Eva Burkholder, December 13, 2016.

2 Scot McKnight, *The Real Mary: Why Evangelical Christians Can Embrace the Mother of Jesus* (Brewster, MA: Paraclete Press, 2007), 7–9.

3 Jane Austen, *Pride and Prejudice* (London, England: Penguin Books Ltd, 1813) Penguin Popular Classics, 1994, 243.

4 Unless otherwise noted, all Greek and Hebrew meanings taken from "Strong's Greek Lexicon (NIV)" or "Strong's Hebrew Lexicon (NIV)." Blue Letter Bible. www.blueletterbible.org/.

5 Darrell L. Bock, *IVP New Testament Commentary Series: Luke* (Downers Grove, IL: InterVarsity Press, 1994) 40.

6 Pete Briscoe, "Who are you in the Story?" *Telling the Truth Experiencing Life* (blog), September 7, 2018, www.tellingthetruth.org/read/individual-post/read/2018/09/07/who-are-you-in-the-story-/.

7 Paul David Tripp, *Suffering: Gospel Hope When Life Doesn't Make Sense* (Wheaton, IL: Crossway, 2018), 92.

8 Vine, Unger & White, *New Testament*, 109, biblehub.com/greek/1096.htm/.

9 Sarah Klitenic Wear, "Wishing for God's Plan: Mary's Fiat in Luke 1:38," *First Things* (blog), December 8, 2015, www.firstthings.com/web-exclusives/2015/12/wishing-for-gods-plan-marys-fiat-in-luke-138/.

10 "Greek Verbs Help Tutorial," Blue Letter Bible, www.blueletterbible.org/help/greekverbs.cfm#intro/.

11 James Prather, "Paul's Profanity," *Think Hebrew* (blog), February 19. 2010, https://thinkhebrew.wordpress.com/2010/02/19/pauls-profanity/.

12 Jackie Roese, *I'm Enough: Learning to Live Confidently in Your Own Skin* (Addison, TX: HIS Publishing Group, 2018), 94.

13 McKnight, 15. "In the 1980s the government of Guatemala banned any public reading of Mary's Magnificat because it was deemed politically subversive … In countries whose citizens lack the basic liberties to say what they think, worship as they want, and to acquire basic needs, a bold plea for justice is an act of subversion."

14 James Bryan Smith, *The Good and Beautiful Life: Putting on the Character of Christ* (Downers Grove, IL: InterVarsity Press, 2009), 57.

15 Smith, 62.

16 Carolyn Custis James, *Lost Women of the Bible: The Women We Thought We Knew* (Grand Rapids, MI: Zondervan, 2007), 35–37. *Ezer* is the Hebrew word that most versions translate as "helper." It appears twenty-one times as a noun in the Old Testament. Sixteen of those references are for God himself who comes as a strong warrior to the aid of his people in need and never as a subordinate inferior. A study of these passages reveals the imagery of battle and thus why the descriptor *ezer warrior* is appropriate.

17 James, 177.

18 Dr. Timothy Ralston, "The Virgin Mary: Reclaiming our Respect," in *Vindicating the Vixens: Revisiting Sexualized, Vilified, and Marginalized Women of the Bible*, edited by Sandra Glahn. (Grand Rapids, MI: Kregel, 2017), 105.

19 "Maternal Mortality," World Health Organization, February 16, 2018, www.who.int/en/news-room/fact-sheets/detail/maternal-mortality/.

20 Michael Kruger, "5 Popular Misconceptions About the Christmas Story," *The Gospel Coalition* (blog), December 20, 2017, www.thegospelcoalition.org/article/5-popular-misconceptions-christmas-story/. See also Taylor Drummond, "Debunking 8 Common Christmas Story Myths," *Patheos* (blog), December 17, 2016, www.patheos.com/blogs/chorusinthechaos/debunking-8-common-christmas-story-myths/.

21 *Anne with an E*, "Remorse Is the Poison of Life." Season one, episode six. Directed by Paul Fox. Created by Moira Walley-Beckett. Based on the novel *Anne of Green Gables* by Lucy Maud Montgomery. Netflix original, April 23, 2017.

22 Carolyn Custis James, *Malestrom: Manhood Swept into the Currents of a Changing World* (Grand Rapids, MI: Zondervan, 2007), 167.

[23] "Where was Joseph when Jesus was an adult?" *Got Questions* (blog), updated July 19, 2019, www.gotquestions.org/Joseph-Jesus.html/.

[24] Ralston, 112-113.

[25] Joseph H. Hellerman, When the Church Was a Family: Recapturing Jesus's Vision for Authentic Christian Community (Nashville, TN: B&H Academic, 2009), chapter 2.

[26] James, *Lost Women of the Bible*, 176.

[27] "When did Mary die?" *Got Questions* (blog) updated July 26, 2019, www.gotquestions.org/when-did-Mary-die.html/.

Acknowledgments

I wish to say thank you to so many who helped make this book a reality.

First, to Joan Dorman who cried, "Book, book," when she read my blog.

To my readers, for taking time to read the draft and give me helpful feedback and encouragement: Mark Burkholder, Suzi Ciliberti, Sue Eenigenburg, Barbara Evans, Karen Dubert, Lula Filbert, Deb Hinkel and Wendy Wilson.

To my editors who combed over every word and made my thoughts so much clearer and correct: Beth Barron for believing that I had something worth sharing, Michelle Rayburn and Linda Revel for your attention to detail.

To my cover artist who paints beautiful watercolors but is actually a great friend and prayer partner who shares Indonesia with me: Lula Filbert. See her gorgeous work at spiceislandoriginals.com and purchase your own print of Mary of Nazareth.

To my cover designer who took Lula's painting and turned it into a real book, Michelle Rayburn missionandmedia.com.

To my ministry partners, my colleagues, my friends, my Tuesday morning Bible study—all who prayed, asked me how the book was coming along, and told me they couldn't wait to read it. You have kept me going.

To my writing groups, WordGirls (kathycarltonwillis.com/wordgirls) and Flourish Writers (flourishwriters.com) who introduced me to the world of publishing and encouraged me to go for it!

To my pastors and the authors who have shed light on the strong and powerful women of the Bible. Without you, I would not have taken a fresh look at Mary of Nazareth.

To my parents who did not live to see their daughter become an author, but I know would be proud and excited. Watching them pore over every verse in the New Testament and give their lives to ensure that the *Biangai* and the *Saposa* people of Papua New Guinea had the New Testament in their native tongue instilled in me a love for God's living Word.

To my husband, Mark, the other half of my beautiful blessed alliance, without whom I would not have learned many of the truths from Mary's life. Thank you for reading every word and giving me honest and helpful feedback. Thank you for encouraging me to fly and for modeling true partnership to our sons. May there be many more like you (and Joseph) in the coming generations.

And lastly,

> "Glory to God in the highest,
> And on earth peace, goodwill toward men!"
> (Luke 2:14)

About the Author

Eva Burkholder was born to missionary Bible translators in Papua New Guinea and later became a global worker herself in Indonesia.

She first began writing stories of life and work for her newsletter, then for church publications, and finally started her own blog, *Pondered Treasures* (evaburkholder.com).

She uses her MA in Christian Education, her training and experience as a women's ministry director, and as a Bible college adjunct professor to enhance her study of Scripture, her writing, and her teaching.

She and her husband currently live in Richardson, Texas, and oversee the wellbeing of global workers for a church planting mission agency. They have two sons and one daughter-in-law.

Eva rejuvenates by doing puzzles, crafting, baking, and sitting by the ocean when she gets the chance. She can be heard strategically quoting lines from Jane Austen, Tolkien, and Star Wars.

Made in the USA
Middletown, DE
14 November 2022

14980470R00086